A Year of Prayers

A Year of Prayers

JACK BARTLETT

RESOURCE *Publications* · Eugene, Oregon

A YEAR OF PRAYERS

Copyright © 2011 Jack Bartlett. All rights reserved. Except for brief quotations in critical publications or reviews, no part of this book may be reproduced in any manner without prior written permission from the publisher. Write: Permissions, Wipf and Stock Publishers, 199 W. 8th Ave., Suite 3, Eugene, OR 97401.

Resource Publications
An Imprint of Wipf and Stock Publishers
199 W. 8th Ave., Suite 3
Eugene, OR 97401
www.wipfandstock.com

ISBN 13: 978-1-61097-337-3

Manufactured in the U.S.A.

All scripture quotations, unless otherwise indicated, are taken from the Holy Bible, New International Version®, NIV®. Copyright ©1973, 1978, 1984 by Biblica, Inc.™ Used by permission of Zondervan. All rights reserved worldwide.

Dedicated to my loving wife, Sandra.

Contents

Foreword ix

1. January 1
2. February 21
3. March 39
4. April 59
5. May 75
6. June 93
7. July 109
8. August 127
9. September 147
10. October 165
11. November 183
12. December 203

Foreword

THE TWO OLDEST BOOKS in this author's personal library are a *King James Bible* given to me when I was a teenager, and a tattered copy of Walt Whitman's *Leaves of Grass*. The Bible was my first book and had been a gift from my sister. Whitman's masterpiece I obtained as a freshman in college. These two books were among the first that I owned and they influenced me significantly, the Bible because it was, well, the Bible, and *Leaves of Grass* because it spoke so much about nature, about the joy and wonder of realization, both of the self and the glorious natural world.

Through my years as a painter of outdoor landscapes, I continued in my interest of poets who addressed the subject of nature and beauty, especially Wordsworth, Frost, and Keats. I became a joyous reader of poetry, particularly those poets whose works used the sound of words and phrases that magnified a sentence rather than merely described an event or feeling; poets like Wallace Stevens, ee. cummings, Theodore Roethke, and especially, Gerard Manley Hopkins and William Blake.

In Hopkins I saw a merging of my own interests in word play, importance of nature, rhythm, and most of all, faith. In most of the poets I read, however, I found scant efforts to unite verse with Scripture, in fact, almost an avoidance of it.

With my faith growing more and more as I grew older, I developed an interest in trying to merge faith and Scripture with verse in some fashion, beginning with poetic salutations to nature and making an effort to elicit my faith as a witness to it. I concluded from my personal reading that there was not enough poetry written that could stand on its own equally as poetry and devotion. There was certainly no shortage of visual artists like Caravaggio, Rembrandt, Tanner and, yet again, William Blake, who had expressed great Scriptural reference in their works. I decided to embark on such a challenging task to combine the two interests, poetry and prayer. I undertook the task of writing and collecting 365 poems that were also prayers, and was humbled and sometimes thought I would never complete all of them.

There were other motives at work in writing this collection of prayer/poems. At the end of the 20th Century I became aware that more than a new century and millennium was nearing. Considering the cultural history of the first ten years of the 20th Century, when all assumptions old and pre-modern were reassessed, in the late 1990's I wondered if the time had come to do the same with the century then ending. I assumed that a similar reassessment of modernism would begin, so I began my own personal evaluations, as much as I could. I planned to examine the cultural and spiritual nostrums of the century, and I considered it my duty to be critical. Of course, anyone could agree that the 20th Century produced the greatest advances in human life expectancy, technology and quality of life, at least in terms of comfort, in the history of mankind. I was convinced that 1999, in many ways, was more unlike 1899 than 1899 was to 899. I also speculated that the last century may have lost as much as it gained, and its most damaging loss was the loss of faith. It saddened me to learn that over 100 million people had been killed in that century by generally those who had left God out of the human equation. These facts were very revealing, and to me, cast suspicion over the nature of our entire recent past. This century needed a hard critique that had seldom been forthcoming, and the postmodern culture we now find ourselves in should have been called the "postponing" culture, one that to me had either denied or postponed the obvious, that indeed mankind is incapable of living without God.

So I began collecting my own prayers in search of finding a voice that heralded God's handiwork in all things, and to do this in the medium of poetry. In doing so, I taught myself how to pray in a new, different manner, attempting to express my own daily devotions in poetic form, and hoping to speak to whomever would listen.

Once I aspired in this direction, the content of what I wanted to express flowed freely and I found my inspiration in Scripture, in worship, dreams, on my own front porch, and in the wonderful natural world in which we all have the privilege to live. My life's love and I have had the pleasure to live where we could see God's grandeur every day. She seconded my notion and encouraged me onward.

I have written this collection with no specific Christian denomination or theology in mind and in fact, have tried to present it as accessible to all Christians and people of faith. It is my hope that in reading the prayer/poems the reader will take as much delight in reading as I did in writing them.

1

January

1. A Year of Prayers

Father,
I offer you a year of prayer
a journey born of gratitude
in celebration of joy,
a daily map towards heaven.

Lord, help me with my bread,
employ the source, the yeast,
help me to aptly leaven
the daily stead, the stuff of days,
help me toward rightful ways,
regardless of critique from others,
save me from the woeful tides
of current conglomerates of conscience,
save me from the folly of persistent sways
that pull me to wrongful passages.

Lord, save me from false myths
and maladies, and of course
keep me true and fresh, untainted
by the strains of unrighteous force,
keep me focused on that which indicates,
confirms, that our lives are more than
brief appearances before we meet
a cold and meaningless dirt.

2. Lamb's Life, Whale's Eye

Lord,
This is the second day on a long march.
I want you to lead me into the New Jerusalem
so that I may live the right way,
that I may find something,
make something to celebrate, every day.
Lead me past struggles dogs and men make
in their circles to make their beds.
Let those who fight cease conflict with each other,
and let me make my way to beauty instead,
to your bounty, so that I may render it.
Show me the lamb's life and the whale's eye,
the salamander's slime, the weave of the unobserved.

Keep my body up to the task
of offering evidence of your treasure.
Keep my heart soft and full of charity,
Satan safely behind his mask, his deeds a rarity,
and keep my children from harm's way.
Amen.

3. Your Rubric Done

Lord,
Thank you for bringing me across
the living river
to be like the locked and loaded
spring that bounces back from dormancy to efficacy
at the proper arc of the sun,
not fooled by temperatures
where it may be jilted by frosts, lose its fruit,
but from a rule, your rubric done.

Thank you for welcoming me back
into the going, gangly, greening,
preening buds to blooms,
ants to elephants, seeds to Sequoias,
eggs to feathers, flights,

from a precipice where the body toils,
where some cells secede and mutiny,
to a fertile valley of your grace
that illuminates the weary nights.

4. O What a Joy

O what a joy
the mockingbird brings,
he has no reason,
no script or instructions
for what he does when he sings.

O what a joy
the music that is
the ear's muse,
our own internal drum,
the blood's fuse.

O what a joy
April brings,
when frost is lost
and in soggy soils
the mushroom springs.

O what a joy
my love in morning's light,
combing her hair, coffee handed,
looking out over the lake with sun through the pines,
clear, certain, bright.

5. What the Katydid Did

O Lord,
I can talk, I can sing,
I can think and walk and love,
with gifts given by you since I was a kid.
I can pray and I can dance,
I can hope, cry and remember,
but I can't do
what the katydid just did.

You gave him wings light as air,
you gave him a pair,
to float and fly across this yard,
and long grasshopper legs so he can jump
like he jumped when I tried to catch him
when I was just a kid,
the way he just jumped, that katydid did.

6. Father, Thank You

Father, from foibles wide and sure,
when I am in retreat,
dodging dangers ever there,
thank you for my feet.

Father, with full fall blue,
when I look up at skies,
nights with your glittering lights,
thank you for my eyes.

Father, for the beat that begins
in embryonic soup from the start
and ends on our last day,
thank you for my heart.

Father, some spans are struggles,
you make demands,
ours is to work for charity, faith, hope,
thank you for my hands.

Father, for our minute-made eternal,
ceasing silence for endless years,
you gave us our own made music,
thank you for my ears.

Father, for the Bard's wonderful words,
voices whispered, spoken, written, sung,
in words, music, verse, my speech,
thank you for my tongue.

7. AS MANY

As many as the leaves on trees,
as many as the stars,
cars on freeways,
as ants crawling,
snowflakes falling,
as many as embers of forest fires,
we send our prayers to you,
O Lord,
usually not for ourselves
but for others, not for our desires
but for your holy healings, and so,
I send this one to you, O Lord,
so you will know
he needs your help very much.
He's only five and his breath is labored,
free him Lord,
and release him of his sickness,
the way you do so many times
with your simple touch.

I pray to you,
I pray for her, for him, for me,
for in our earthly durations we
are like new nest birds
with our mouths wide open,
waiting for mother mana
to enter our needy throats,
we, who suffer and weep,
unable to fly, who reap
your bounties and give praise
but sooner or later need
your hand, as he does now.

8. Ephphatha

Lord Jesus,
To heavens obscured by pasty grays,
eyes vacant of currents, hues,
ears vibration-spared, held captive to still tyrannies of silence,
hearts with holes without counterparts,
feet lost on paths through desert wastes without water,
you would say, "be thou open".

To those confined to chairs, beds,
dry wicks without oil, no light shed on wicked ways,
tongues unable to finesse a voice locked in moist mouths
the way pearls are oyster-locked in deep sea shells,
cold lips, empty hands secreted in pockets,
windows closed that could allow light
to seduce the cornea with yellow lust,
to doors that shut out ways and means,
winter woods weaned of springs,
you would say "be thou open".

Tractions lose to plasma mud,
gelatin blood in vascular streams,
durable days diminishing,
with crimson stolen from the rose
and allergens prowl the house like ghosts,
to those in beds, rocked, endless pain days as though
their torsos were snake-wrapped, serpent–seized,
whose leg-iron steps look as though they're there to stay,
to those who have no where to go,
to all of the above,
you would say, "be thou open".
   From Mark, 7:34

9. Into the Tangle of Your Doings

Over the hills and through the woods
I crawl through rhododendron bramble,
through thick briars,
across mountain streams

where little brownies
hide under rocks the size of refrigerators,
stepping over velvet moss, oozing springs,
into the tangle of your doings,
into a private sanctum where creatures scramble
with their creature wooings,
where no one has ever visited
except for me and you, O Lord.

There, as sure as in any grand cathedral,
I stop and sit,
and am sure I have found
my holy church fit
for kings and commoners alike,
into the tangle of your doings,
O Lord.

10. The Pitchfork of the Devil

Lord,
We are here
and we know where that is,
we know where we are
and where we've been,
we're in a new century and millennium
and we remember the last,
when many more were harmed
by those who didn't believe in you
than by those who did.
So, let's start a new path,
reject the old,
accept again that beauty is truth,
and ugliness is the pitchfork
of the devil.

11. Here's To

Lord Jesus,
Here's to what shouldn't have happened, and did,
what should not be, but is,
to all efforts at good fortune
and effortless tragedy.

Here's to your glass woods,
made crystalline by winter's icy assertion,
when all in silence remember
what could have been, and not.

Here's to what should be, and isn't,
through all the frozen wants
and below zero haunts
of the day before and today.

Here's to my time,
my own and only time,
I know it by the sound
of the dog's frosty barks down the way.

Here's to all that never comes and all that always goes
without control, without warning,
through the trees where the wind and dog growl,
through the air where the snow blows.

12. This Year of Prayers

I'm on my marathon in prayer
to you, O Lord,
I've just posted my twelfth mile,
along with praise, gratitude,
and cannot see the end in sight.

I will finish if I might
have you to continue to supply me
with needs, seeds of prayer,
peace that comes with your blessings.

I ask that now in your name, Lord,
you protect my family from all grief,
to let me run my race
toward completion, toward you,
that I may have recorded
this year of prayers.

13. Wick Me Up

Wick me up
O Lord, into your spirit,
the way clay lamps wicked oil
for your people in the dark Roman catacombs,
the way the soil wicks water
to nourish roots after rain,
the way those who believe in you
are wicked onto you in death,
the way our lungs wick oxygen
into our blood, our need,
your blood in joy or pain,
again and again,
the way your spark wicks the seed
into life from a wickless cell.

14. How Can I Keep From Weeping?

O Lord,
When I'm in your house
my soul is never sleeping,
it bursts with love and flows forth,
it feels your presence
among the others,
how can I keep from weeping?

Father, in your house
we are at our best,
we do not strive to win but mostly be,
we seek not treasure for our keeping,
we share your spirit ever giving,
how can I keep from weeping?

O Lord,
We sing your praise,
your grace lands on us like a bird
on the shoulder of Saint Francis,
all of us have heard
your word and felt your suffering,
we are here, salvation we are seeking,
through stained glass windows the light is breaking,
how, from joy, can I keep from weeping?

15. If So, A Hope

Father,
We begin, thrust into bright lights
with our grape sized hearts,
plum sized brains,
eyes that mimic the blind,
pea sized fingers, hands pre-wrinkled.
We expand exponentially, grow hair,
encounter lust, loss,
sometimes find dry holes,
sometimes gold, get old,
eyes mimic blind again,
inner ears cannot amplify
and there music goes to die,
our bones saddle-creak,
our muscles like old leather,
toes like sea shells,
hands still wrinkled not steady,
we slow, then stop, so,
this is how it ends,
why play if no one wins,
why not nothing but what pleases self?
How can we possibly cope?
Either a reason for the day or not, in you,
if so, a hope.

16. The P & W Brothers

Lord,
The p & w brothers are
power and wealth,
they share the same DNA,
they are co-joined and cannot exist
apart from each other, any day,
they are roost rulers
at their given time and place,
and are in positions only artists share,
being viewed best by history,
long after memories dim,
long after their appeal has died,
long after their pinnacle has passed,
the lens of the ages examine them,
and so do you.

17. I Fly

Twirling and turning in the widening lair,
surrounded by bramble and honeybee buzzing,
equipped with lacy thin dragonfly wings,
I pray and rise above the early air,
above the bramble and angled span.

I fly, low, the tangle of intentions below,
surveying what was done and not,
marveling at the brightest hour,
the radial purple passion flower,
dismissing times when hope is rotten,
joy jaded, almost faded,
instead heap concentrations
on the flight itself, brief in its fuse,
grateful in the heightened wing,
grateful for your gift, divine muse,
O Lord.

18. Maker

Lord of creation,
You have made something that had to be made
and could not be randomly endowed
with its helix constructions,
not made like curvilinear dunes shaped by wind
or water carved canyons
but still arrived at by purpose
and allowed all to listen to your plan
or else become endangered.
Sometimes even listeners become victims
of something else planned.

Every leaf is its own
and not like any other grows green,
forest tapestry a handiwork
laid down in each cellular organism,
trying to expand, to survive.

Lord, Maker of global grit and rot,
you keep the alpha and omega humming,
on rocks your turtles are sunning,
on desert sand your lizards running,
please keep this hand attesting,
and not let me not be. Amen.

19. A Cardinal Kiss

Lord God,
Almighty clockmaker,
holy engineer of all
that knows what to do, even
the male cardinal knows
his mate needs seeds,
he delivers one to her,
beak to beak
like a kiss at our feeder,
so that for him
there's nothing else to seek
except seeds and his cardinalness.

Lord you allowed the hawk to know
the sweetness of a crawfish,
you taught him to be an opportunist
just like you taught the rabbit
to be an escape artist,
the way you taught the copperhead
to be stealth, resemble leaves,
and always be aware of fire ants.
You taught the fire ants to be
viruses with legs.

But you, O Lord,
left us to our own devices,
and the chance to know what
copperheads and fire ants do not know,
but should I stray,
should I strive and miss,
Lord, please deliver to me
a springtime cardinal kiss.

20. Should We?

Father, should many of us in deed and song,
strive to amass a record
that will last, endure like quarried stone,
one that indicates we lent
something to the days, ways, wishes of others?
Should we care if we are remembered
after we are gone?

Should we work to build a light
that flickers after our heat,
when people may say, "this is the chair where he sat"
or at least say something?
Should we care about our time
before you come for us,
should we even consider that?

Many who lived before where there is now
nothing but pebble, rock and ruin
have done their all to pass on
a word, way or song,
Judeans, Greeks, Apostles all,
should we emulate them, and if so, how?

21. Your Eternal Giving

The snow tiptoes through the air,
quiet brush strokes that paint
the spaces white,
as if to say, "I am winter, behold me."

The snow is for the pines a trimming,
a manicuring of what should not be.
We are hoping our snowman
makes it through the day.
There, a dead branch falling from a tree,
whose limbs are two-toned.

Snowflakes manifest themselves
silently, shortly living,
icy laced, weightless,
all unique, arranged by
your electron magic giving
to us, O Lord.

22. Back Among the Trees

Lord,
I'm back among January woods,
the trees your father's skeleton,
the forest the hair of the earth body
and you are in your place,
the eye sees the rest of the body
but the body does not see the face.

I've been among the wheels and pavement
but now I'm walking in puddly water
along the scalp of the earth,

under the land's fingers
that reach up toward you, with you.

I'm back among black clouds
the color of burning tire smoke
and the sky a night chocolate blue,
the color of the eyes
tonight, Lord, of you.

23. THE THIRD EAR

Father,
You gave us a third ear
that hears what is not said,
that listens between lines and words
and does not often miss,
swords of danger tucked between promises
of those who deceive us with a smile
instead of a kiss.

We can imagine this:
that we can hear untruths
with their always disguised voices,
we can hear only what others hear
and what devilish mouths want us to know,
but there is another way,
we do have choices,
but only if we perceive in silent memory
the consequences of what deceivers say
and only if we hear
with senses attuned, sharpened, alerted,
with your gift to us, our third ear.

24. OUR KINGDOM ON THE LAKE

In our kingdom on the lake,
yellow light after rain delights
with color doubling between glows,
a vacation from the ordinary,
with the woodsy extraordinary,

with its washing away of troubling
times and places,
the pinks too are off to the races,
the storm has shot its wad
and we are free for goodness sake,
in our kingdom on the lake.

25. Maker of All That Is, Was, or Will Be.

Maker, make me over again to help
me reach those who deny you,
those who continue with their mischievous designs
on wealth and power,
those who disintegrate into dust
at the end of their quests, with death
being the final end of hope,
life, love, loved ones, and all held dear,
even their wealth and power
and their lives fade into memory
that becomes faint as weak tea,
until not even memory is left,
for there is no power that comes from the grave
other than yours.

26. Down the River in My Boat

Down the river in my boat,
riding my own wake,
gliding on currents,
passing shoals, eddies, deep holes,
have traveled a ways so far,
trusting in you for your sake.

Down the river in my boat,
have got the wind at my back,
a breeze on the lea,
have passed stragglers,
been passed by speedsters, Lord,
who have ignored you and will surely
be disappointed when the river
straightens and runs into the sea.

Down the river in my boat,
I'm thankful for the water, Lord,
grateful for the ride,
not fearful of the next bend,
not fearful of falls,
rocks, logs in my path,
not fearful when I reach
the ocean's turquoise tide.

27. A Bank of Gratitudes

I live in paper pages
like a worm does in the soil,
I am making up, launching
my prayers to you, O Lord.
I am building a body of solicitations,
making up my own oil,
sending out my invitations,
creating a bank of gratitudes,
an auditing of my faith
in you, O Lord.

28. Be There

Father, my father,
be there with the quarter moon smile,
pale too upon pale blue,
with light spent cycles ruptured in darkness,
there with exhausted winds
and the lake white-vinyl still,
there with the mallard's final wake
when all birds have abandoned concert.

Be there, shadow caster, time allotment master
whose swish is sweeter and makes
the best of painters' brushes sway with envy.
Show your hand slowly,
but still, so, let me sense it.

Father, be there,
you don't have to show it,
as long as I know it,
I'm fine without a sign,
as long as you are there.
Amen.

29. A Grain of Wheat

Lord,
Unless a grain of wheat falls to the ground and dies
there can be no more wheat to eat
unless a flower sends its pollen away
there can be no more flowers,
unless a fish releases its eggs from within
there can be no more fishes,
unless a single bean must sprout and die
there can be no more beans,
and unless you had died for us
there could be no more life after our death.

30. The Slivers

Lord,
Someone stole our pedigree
that at its zenith,
like a gentle dog did not
attack others.

They took away our stock
in increments they invoked,
much like your St. Sebastian moments,
much like your suffering seen
in paintings by the masters,
the slivers seen of cut flesh
you first endured.

They took away our pedigree,
that was reborn in 1776
by men and women who

believed in you and that by
that belief thought their land would be blessed,
more by you than by anything they could do.

Lord,
Obedience was their brand,
one taken away by ages of slivers
from the wickedness some possess
then and now,
from those who put themselves
and their man-made ideas
ahead of you, and use you
as a false badge of their authenticity.

31. This Breathing Life

Lord,
Mostly I come to you in prayer
for others, for her, the one without another,
without an ear or reciprocal love,
for the sick, the lost,
the left without, the confused, empty,
but tonight I come to you for me,
to guide me past that which
could take me from this breathing life.

2

February

32. Was That You?

    Father,
    Was that you moving the lilies
    at the altar last Sunday?
    They moved as if touched by a wind,
    but wind doesn't blow inside a room,
    so was that you sneaking into our spiritual nest,
    just as we were all confessing our sin,
    all of us at our very best?

    Was that you dancing with the candle flame
    that flickered and threatened to go out,
    a candle beside the lilies, red orange against the white?
    Was that you showing your hand with fire,
    a moving, feeble light?
    So that those of us who were paying attention
    knew that you were there,
    trying to take us onward,
    on to a breath without a body,
    trying to take us forward, toward you, higher.

    Was that you,
    that gentle wind in the trees that sway,
    the wind that cools the shadows
    on a steamy summer day?
    Was that your breath, a soothing message from you
    that moves the grains of wheat?

The devil has a breath too,
and when it comes it breaks
the tall trees in two,
it rips and rages, destroying the old,
makes nothing new.
Father, thank you for your breath
that relieves us from the summer heat.

33. The Other Side of This

One day I will close my eyes
and go to sleep,
and fall into the arms of you
O Lord, in bliss,
and will know then what none
of the living now know,
what's on the other side of this.

One day I will leave
to not return here,
and be in the company of those
who've already made the journey,
who met the pledge to believe,
that there is something other than
the body where the cardiac engine hums,
the venal plumbing runs red,
the oxygen collector absorbs the air,
brings life to a run of suns, moons,
day in, day out, even in sleep,
with never a miss,
until all is silent
on the other side of this.

34. He Will Rest in Peace

Lord,
He dies but lives on in you.
Tomorrow as winter is resting
from its rock-hard grip,
and spring's fruit the birds are not yet nesting,

he will be put into the ground
but like the March buds and blooms
we remember in the snow,
we will remember him and all those
he prayed over at their graves, and so,
a fine pastor leaves us, his just release
to your grand pastoral paradise.
Lord, you are receiving one of your servants.
There is no doubt he will rest in peace.

35. The Beatitudes

Lord Jesus,
In the Beatitudes you told us
that those who hunger and thirst
for righteousness will be filled.
So, should we a life our own desires pursue
to only our strong headed motives willed,
and if we think we are not poor in spirit,
are not merciful and meek,
should our own fulfillments
be the only thing we seek,
we will have ignored what you told us, too,
how we should live while we are here
breathing, our feet on the ground,
should we not obey
we will not find you,
nor will we be found.
    From: Matthew 5:3–11

36. Fantasies Absent of You

Father,
It should be apparent after twenty centuries,
especially the last one,
that we have more to fear
from those who deny you and your son,
with hearts cold as river stone,
with over one hundred million killed
in the last century alone,

have we not learned anything
from the past, from a cruel legacy fulfilled,
about just what produces peace, love,
liberty, and at least a possibility of harmony?
Have we not learned that
there are those who continue to make excuses
for the failures of fantasies
that are absent of you?

37. Blood of the Martyrs

Lord,
The blood of the martyrs
was red water for your tree
and the more your enemies shed it
the larger your tree grew,
they never knew
that, given all your martyrs had to do
was disavow you
and by not doing so,
increased their numbers,
recruiting your enemies in all the ages since.
O Lord, should we have their faith today.

38. Light on the Ground

Went looking for your lordly leafy fire, Father,
burnt bloomed ghosts of expansions
in mansions of unobserved growth,
free from ruin or costly loss
where just past ever watchful eyes
a bud swells, a cocoon cracks,
a mushroom parts the moss.

Went looking for woodsy blood breaking into shower,
candy cones of dancing colors imagined,
for possums and finches, ebullient sound,
conifer canopied streams,
elephant rocks, hemlock clusters, bear scat,
found only light on the ground.

Went looking for whatever was there,
evidence of rocky crush, seismic change,
time's grind, seasonal doors,
Dios dust evident yet not obvious,
fallen hawk feathers on fertile forest floors,
or to see my face in still river water.

Went looking for mile marker, direction,
confirmation, tree ring telling, divine sign,
stone clues, the forest's broken secret,
shielded sun held by veil of fog,
blue shade, cricket choir,
ebony night sky, moon round,
looked back and forth, up and down,
in valleys, hollows, steep fern fields,
found only light on the ground,
and gave thanks to you, O Lord.

39. Your Worldly Lair

Father, two millennia have passed
since you were taken from us,
and those who took you are still here,
but we must love them as you did
because your father's justice
is beyond our understanding.
We should love not in fear nor make our bid
for anger at those who deny you, instead,
Lord, pray for them.

The world goes on with all of us in tow,
making the same mistakes,
flesh bound, shackled by our foibles,
our sin the fish's roe,
lacking in eternal trust that you are always there
bursting seed, cracking bud and egg,
making the mother motor run,
each cycle giving all life the nurturing sun
to all the creatures in your worldly lair.

40. Wine in a Cup

Lord Jesus, should I be like the dishonest judge
and be diligent in my petitions to you?
If I hold my hands up in prayer
will you award me the way
Moses was blessed against Amakek?
Will you be my shade in the searing sun,
my ferry across dark waters,
when my race is run?

Will you hold me up
the way buttresses did cathedral walls?
Lord, even though we cannot make
an equation, a correlation between
our prayers and our answers to them,
the prayers are enough in that I know
that answers are not always
as evident as wine in a cup.
      From: Exodus 17:8–13, Timothy 3:14, Psalms 121:1–8

41. Broken Promise

Lord, I promised to polish the moon
on nights corroded by clouds,
not casting broth-thin shadows
when moon emulated sun,
when runs of ruddy space had passed,
but failed, too much, too soon.

I promised to not look past four seasons' feasts,
ruby reds divided between trees
in dusky hours that dissolved away
the pinky east at ten degrees,
I pledged to praise but failed.

Like most promise breakers
I intended to keep such for tomorrow,
postponing somehow,
delaying laying credit to you, O Lord,

a contract like most fakers to duty made,
not knowing penalties that grow
like sludge in foul fields, until now.

Father, forgive my silly slips of honor,
for baths in crazy oil, laps of lazy strain,
not sensing pure pine scent, juniper rain,
blessed bearings in full view I chose to eschew,
orchard prize, wavy ways in windy March,
dirt eggs that bloom, pumpkinseed bream,
solace of an August shade, iced tea under a holly tree.
Forgive and I will recommit, I promise.

42. All I Need to Know

Abba, I am your heir,
one of your many adopted sons,
a member of your extended family
with all your other sons and daughters, so
I consider them brothers and sisters,
together we all believe in you, your father and spirit,
and that is all I need to know.

43. Your Rain Makes

Lord, your rain's better than what
it keeps me from doing,
with singing silvers, looming sways
of pelleted wind, leaves breathing relief sighs,
the skies with gravy grays.

Your rain's piano music for fishes,
scaly wishes fulfilled,
gilled mouths ready for watery runs
in mountain springs brownies rejoice,
newts ecstatically lounge on rocks.

Your rain's background armadillo music,
snooty noses ready for the root,
they wait in dirt holes until dark,
with the ground then like wet grits.

Your rain's almighty saliva
that moistens earthen mouths.
Birds hide from it, don't dislike it,
knowing it makes insects into drunkards.

Your rain shapes rocks, soil, hillsides, grasses,
determines what is or won't be,
a creek bank fern, tropical tree
trying to grow in Alamogordo,
a cactus in a Florida swamp.

Your rain makes hills and dissolves them,
makes wildflowers, drizzling hours, springs, rivers,
and when it says no
changes their courses or yellows their livers,
then jaundiced currents carry their loads
downstream into big brown arteries,
onward, snaking away to seas.

Your rain makes all except, in its absence desert dust,
feeds the big body mundi,
slurries the skies, hides the stars.
O how the dried river beds must
pine in memory of what once was
along burnt orange crevasses of Mars.

44. Consequently, Miss This

Father,
At dawn fog falling,
trees drip with opaque dew,
morning is born among the branches
as it always has,
another vestige of you,
presents like the dog by my side,
deer moving among old shadows
at first light before the wind breathes.

But there have always been
those who oppose this and you,
who lobby for largess, lassitude
of spirit, ambivalent to true blood
even Aztecs could smell, faith fortitude
in this liquid/solid tissue stew,
oil of is, vapored charge,
those who spend their lives on that,
and consequently miss this.

45. Spring Will Be Soon

Father of the natural world,
the hawks are letting us know,
on this lake, this cove,
that this is their space, no other,
and they have felt surely now,
on this cold February day they see,
that spring will be soon,
the clocks that you gave them are ticking,
they are flying from tree to tree,
investigating, picking on time, steadily
the perfect spot to build a nest,
the cardinals too and all the rest,
must see the signaling of the daffodils
and know that the time for mating
will be upon them readily.

46. Dissolving Into You

Lamb of God,
Will we dissolve into you
the way honey does into hot tea,
the way the afternoon is slowly
reduced into evening, the slow slide ways,
the way childhood disappears by days?
Will we realize immediately
that we are becoming you
the way a chrysalis dissolves into flight,
the burning desert day into the cold night?
We wait to be blended with you
now, then, forever.

47. Flesh and Blood

Lord Jesus, I thought it was flesh
but it tasted like a cracker
when I swallowed a portion of the God body,
while outside the sky
was a pale berry blue
and ice was bleaching the green from the trees.

I drank the wine blood,
squeezed from a precious grape,
from a devine vine that left its fruit
for all of us to take.

48. All Will Be Rearranged

Help us, O Lord,
the beasts are loose and fast,
they never sleep and babies
are taken from the womb at last,
some do whatever they want
and have lost any sense of shame,
adults prey on children like fox to bird,
many ignore your word
and there is a coming of the days
when this cannot be sustained.
I know, Lord, these ways
cannot last and all will be rearranged
as it has been in times past.

49. Full Fledged

This is what I wanted in other days,
the steep incline of whirling ways,
on my way to acres of bounty blossomed,
no longer a sprout or sapling but a tree,
full fledged into where you have delivered me.

Please, Lord, let me be
like the big, Joyce Kilmer poplars
rising above Smoky Mountain mist,

or the octopus shaped Mississippi live oak
that was a boy when sails first arrived in the Gulf,
that withstood the full fledged Katrina fist.

Please, Lord, let me be then,
a living elder content to see
the churn of a buttery wish fulfilled,
the glory of light on a rock or knee,
full fledged into the optical spectacle of privileged sight.

To tip the tongue with lime
or sea fruit or both, without dangers, losings, fears,
to taste turmeric, feta and olive, popsicle,
the roux of the spring bud's delight,
I make my wish to you, O Lord,
that I might spread the hours into years.

50. Take Our Tack

Lord, take our tack
and steer us to where
we are supposed to be,
in your beginning of the end
or end of the beginning.

When will we know if we are winning,
Lord, will we have to wait for your return,
or do you plan that we plow
our own furrows,
moving platonic shadows forward,
our own feeble attempts at justice and accountability,
improving on snail slow charts of slow growth
until we are with you?

51. Render Unto Me

Render unto me the red velvety runnings
of sun cycles, untarnished times
when much is given but not much taken away.

Am I being a grace hog,
gluttonous of ephemeral prizes
that announce themselves in unwashed windows,
narcissist quick and without calling?

I'm not asking for a fortune strike
or a mother lode of providence,
a passel of precipitous precious riches,
only that I am left
to present appreciations of blessed breathing,
so I can balance what I cannot see
but can see what I believe.

52. On Your Last Day

Lord,
Give us the strength to defy
the pack that herds the masses
to do what they do,
floating like flotsam downstream,
all in questionable agreement,
often without input from you,
stampeding into collective maladies
they cannot see
the way they did on your last day,
with each wanting to be accepted,
so accepting falsehoods that led
and lead away from you.

Father,
Don't let us go so far
that we can never find our way back.
Don't let our fears of non acceptance
take us to a place of no return,
a place where your truth
is substituted by an absence of any truth
and freewheeled by those in power,
the way they did on your last day.

53. Against the Walls

Lord, you never asked us to be tolerant of evil,
to allow it to use our own devices for its workings,
because it will always seek a way
to penetrate righteous defenses,
to set afire its demonic fuse
amongst the unsuspecting.

We are thin as dragonfly wings
in our open defense,
the holy under assault
from those who wish to do
only what pleases sense,
only what feels good despite
the rupture of the common good,
eternal envelope pushing,
forever pushing against the walls
of your holy might,
forever in denial to what is not
easily discernable in you,
O Lord.

54. Time for Corrections

Lord, Titus built his mighty arch
celebrating Jerusalem's demise,
a monument against you and your kind
with soldiers marching proudly,
in praise of the ruin of the temple
where you sat as a boy among elders.

But you, O Lord,
play a slow hand with time,
letting vain emperors
and vulgar cultures reign, even use
force in defiance of you,
giving them, and us,
ample time to right our tilted boats
and when we refuse,

we are eventually swamped with adversity
we cannot overcome, as with the Romans.
Lord, give us time for corrections.

55. Good Friday

Today is the day you went away, Lord,
taken from the human flock
in a brutal way.
You allowed yourself to be
a fulfillment of prophecy,
the one promised, dreamed of,
but even some of the dreamers still deny you.
You are the smoking gun
of evidence that we are not alone.

If we think we are,
then ours is a lonely station
because we alone among your creatures
ask why we are here,
the much adorned leopard with his spots does not,
neither does the whistling winged dove,
the magnificent raptors with wings for sails,
the streamlined, quiet footed deer,
the many colored tulips that show up
each year like spring color trumpets,
none of which asks what
they are doing here.

But when we seek, we find,
should we have no other clue,
having turned over many rocks
looking, searching, never finding,
until we stand on the rock of you.

56. Psalmist Evermore

Lord,
You turn your back to dust,
to the legions of those who have
come and gone, sprouted from wombs,

spanned their times,
and like newborn grass
is gone in evening and wilts and fades.

You turn your back because
they are among you who have lived
according to your plan,
but not those who have peddled
a living contraband.

You turn your back to ages
and focus on the new,
the now living who cooperate,
Lord, have pity on your servants,
who defy offers to not be a part of you.

Farther, teach us to not run astray,
to not gather up riches and forget
those who do not,
yet in their lives have shown,
wisdom of hearts, ever yet.

57. Easter Day

Lord Jesus,
You alone escaped the boundary
of the black dirt dominion.
You pulled away the cover and flew away
on this blooming, beaming Easter Day.

You rose above this physical limitation,
above perimeters, the nucleus noose,
toward a status with no peers
among the living or the dead.
You proved that spirit precedes body,
dwells within it
yet is not its prisoner
when you abandoned blood and bone
for a place beside your father.

We are here and as a result not alone.
Your example shines above
the dull silence, finite grave with your teaching.
We see you mostly when not looking,
in the wind across a field, the revolving seasons,
the protected turtle, giraffe neck made most for reaching,
infant skin, love's lips, a phone call that announces
our future is now booking.

58. Hover, Father

Holy Father, hover
over me in the endless seeping hours,
hover over the needy masses,
the wind in the blonde grasses,
the bee spreading dust, the lust of flowers,
the bric a brac of breaking pastures
where your presence has stained the fields.

Hover over the measures that make
this breathing's plan,
other than mere breath, in, out,
then silent as an empty sea.
Hover over the single cell,
citadel of sparking fluid,
current of the pulsing row
that flows back in to me.

Holy Father, hover
over all, except the dead, the second rail
who no longer need you like we do as a spark,
hover over each green leaf and king,
from the smallest to the massive,
crustacean to the whale,
hover now and then with all,
between the daylight and the dark.

59. All of the Above

Lord, Isaiah prophesized your birth
from the house of David,
that you were to be virgin born
and that you would be called Emmanuel,
and so, from the beginning
we are asked to accept this,
that you are the Messiah,
that you are the one waited for,
who did not come with arms for war
but with open arms.
We are asked to accept
that your life was designed
from Bethlehem to Golgotha with love,
to accomplish just what you did,
in spite of your suffering.
We accept, Lord,
all of the above.

60. In Solitude, Silence, Prayer

Lord, in solitude, silence, prayer,
transport me to your feet,
so that on my knees
I may kiss them,
transport me to your bubble of peace,
let me know that I am
in the company of your adorers,
flocks of different feathers and colors.

Let us all joy-skip past foot-slippings,
to be like ballerina toes
on a bald man's head,
in perfect balance, weightless
in your liquid air.

O Lord,
In solitude, silence, prayer,
transport me to your peace,
calm as undisturbed mercury
or windless coves of lake water,
a peace whose price of admission,
is not costly 'cept the price
of an honest admitted submission.

3

March

61. The River and the Man

Father, your process begins as a faint flowing, a trickle,
an innocent oozing from crevasses and springs into life,
harboring salamanders, themselves fetus-like
in their dark and protected enclaves.

As a stream your little water pools
and while as an infant the little man
is on his way to becoming,
the stream is on its way to going.

At adolescence the stream deepens
and imitates the river with its fishes,
sand bars, bends and aquatic drama,
while the boy dreams and wishes.

As an adult the river packs its power
to change the valley, to move soil, flood fields
and carry your heaven's rains from its lands,
while at maturity the man holds the strength
of even the rivers in his hands.

Like the river the man bends with age, slowly,
and like it looses his meandering search
to seek and flow and grow free,
and his current too is slow, deep and wise,
snaking its way to the sea.

62. On the Other Side of Here

She ventures now and within
into the kiln that cooks the vessel
that holds the flown spirit that has already landed
and touched blood and bread where
a new traveler waits for shoes and directions.

The traveler inherits the current
of the unending line cast out,
and will burst out into light
in electric communion with other absentees
on the other side of here.
O Lord, bring her in.

63. June Bug

A June bug landed
on my finger in April.
He was whipped, weak from flying
so let me transfer him
from one finger to another too,
and didn't want to let go.
He clung to me like I do to you,
O Lord.

We are many and are in the society of clingers
who never completely understand
but persist and demand
with our charity and our voices,
allegiance to you, Lord, especially,
there being no other sufficient choices.

What has history shown
but foibles millennia old and known,
and references, remembrances
of many who have lived righteous lives
and may they be blessed, whoever they are or were,
but you are the Righteous One,
and in previous times

your opponent's results in human spheres
have been documented, discredited
and from analysis of reason have flown.

Of course there were times
when your would-be clingers misbehaved,
did things contrary to your will,
joined the ranks of the depraved,
but have been exposed
and are with us still.

How do we know that the June bug wasn't
a killer, a destroyer, a bullet bodied stinger
at some time in his woodsy past
but now is a peaceful friend, somehow?
If so, how do we know when
he made his transition?
How do we know when we've made ours?
Can I crawl up your finger, Lord,
and hear you say that it is now?

64. Riding with the Singers

Lord, don't know where the music's taking me,
the rhythm of the sphere,
whines of pines, swish of sage,
wind chant, sea roar that never ceases,
your holy hum that sizzles sound,
massages the audio canal,
all along the hearing tower
that seeks your ever present whispers.

The music disturbs sandy desert dust,
whips water into foam, reaps sound,
sows cadence older than stone all around,
I'm riding with the singers of seasons,
warm summer wind that feathers a wet face,
fall leaf flutter, winter snow
falling quietly as kitten paws on carpet,

spring chorus birds birding, buds bursting,
I'm riding with the singers and praying
all the way home.

65. I Would Choose the Latter

Less of more
is more than more of less,
lest one choose quantity over quality.
Should I choose between
sitting on a porch for a year
drinking iced tea,
or a walk along ancient streets
in Italy,
I would choose the latter.
Should I have to choose between
some other life than the one given
and the one received from you, O Lord,
I would choose the latter.

I dreamed my wife and I
were young again
and had not been visited
by the wrecking ball of age,
we had each other
and our uncorrupted bodies,
but we didn't have you.
Should I be able somehow
to go back to then,
be young, have our futures ahead of us,
or be here now, with you,
I would choose the latter.

66. Larva Dei (Mask of God)

Lord, do you hide yourself from us,
revealing yourself anywhere,
on a porch, plane, produce isle,
on Aventine Hill on a bus?
Do you hide and let our wills just be

until, in avoidance, we
leave you for our own pursuits,
giving us chance after chance
and when we exhaust your offers,
you show up and punish us?

Lord, when you appear
we know you sometimes take
even your own servants
or the young, but to a better place,
you hide from us for our own good
for should your presence be obvious
there would be no need for us
to prove ourselves worthy
of your love and grace.

67. Eggs and Seeds

Father, do you plant a clock inside a seed,
hidden in its DNA a time
when solar geometries are right,
for it to respond to its need
to burst and germinate forth in green delight
and cast its germ into the living?

Do you plant a clock inside an egg,
instructions for it to burst
into a bloom of feathers, an eye, an ear, a leg,
rocketing into being, silently,
until its heart has pumped its allotted runs?

Have you designated a specific number
of days, moons, suns,
for even jackals, worms, weeds,
for the living, growing, moving that begins
with your currency-eggs and seeds?

68. And Dream of You

Lord,
I will keep a lamp
in front of my feet
so that, in daylight
I am reminded of my duty to be
the best of me for your grace,
and at night it will light
the way out of darkness
until I sleep in the dust of the earth
and dream of you.

And the dream, absent of woe,
considering its making,
will be more real than waking, and so,
all will be there, mothers, fathers,
grandpaws and dogs,
and the awake will not know
what we know.
   From Psalms 119:105

69. Bread of Life

Lord,
You are the light on the lily,
alpha omega, chi rho,
crossover piper from death into life,
uncaused first cause,
multiplier of barley loaves and fishes,
water walker, thirst quencher,
bread of life without whose nourishment
the organism eventually perishes,
healer of wounds,
yeast of our hearts
that rise toward your father,
toward the bread that came down from heaven,
that can fall on our shoulders.

70. A Greater Gift

> Lord,
> Ever since that Friday
> when you gave up your treasured gift,
> there have been those who proclaim
> to be "in the know" to describe you
> in ways that lessen your mystery,
> suggesting that you are not of the Father,
> are separate from him,
> or that you were only a man,
> yet, Lord, the rest of us know
> through Scripture and stories
> that you gave your gift of life,
> then three days later a greater gift.
>
> Just as my grandfather told me stories
> of days mostly forgotten but true,
> passed down around talk tables,
> there were those who saw you,
> who saw what you did that had never been done
> before or since, that lift
> of flesh you gave to spirit substance,
> to an irrefutable rising many still deny,
> that mystery you gave on Easter Sunday,
> O Lord, thank you for that gift.

71. They Know What to Do

> Lord,
> They all know what to do
> in your busy byzantine matrix,
> trees perform the way trees are supposed to,
> bass in the water do impersonations
> of little lake sharks,
> all is determined, arranged by you,
> the all-tidy ado,
> all are looking for others
> the way even pear trees do,
> all aligned, planned, smooth,

efficient, such as when the wind
prunes the dead limbs from the trees,
relieving them of memory.

Lord,
How could anyone not see
the harmony in this arrangement
that could have not become itself haphazardly,
that is too ornate for mere chance?
The raccoons' eyes glow in the dark,
it is spring and they know what to do,
more raccoons is their goal,
all according to you.

72. Filled With the Air

My spirit is like a rubber tire,
pumped, filled with air,
buoyant, contented, moving forward
until one day inside there,
I spring a leak
and then admit, confess,
that I have faltered in my faith
and patch the hole
with prayer,
then once again I am puffed,
and filled with the air
of you, O Lord.

73. Your Love, Casually

Lord,
Free the rain from above,
let a soft wetness fill our faces
when we are dry the most,
be the host, make the good excel
above the gloomy traces
of undesirable events,
casually as you do with
long sun arcs across the summer sky,

days extended in width,
burning the grasses and our skin,
let clouds come billowing by
and empty themselves onto our arms below,
let wetness in and there will be others dancing,
even the grasses ever romancing
the green, the trees singing ever so,
as we witness just another episode
of your love, casually.

74. Among the Present

Lord,
Our birth is but a setting
about a span expanding
wider, not narrower we pray,
we watch minute slide
into an hour, then day,
weeks to months to years
and then a life framed, done,
goes, and with most,
a dreadful footnoted forgetting.

Names on registers come and go forever and a day
like passengers in a station, buying tickets
for the geneology express,
anonymous souls buzzing past,
seldom stopping to question
how long their journeys may last,
but along the way beauty shines
and with its cousin faith
are the lamplights of our limited stay
among the present, O Lord.

75. A Field of Mines

Lord,
The meek are weak,
because love can be corrupt,
can be disguised from what it is,
instead, motives the flesh may seek.

None of us are immune
to passions of carnal wants,
or greed from money's lure,
under any sun or moon.

We walk a field of mines,
projected into our faces day and night,
made handsome by the artist's hand,
we stray, we suffer, and pay our fines.

So Satan wears a feathered hat,
is glamorous in his perfumed ways,
we sense nothing but the scent,
are naive in the nature of that,

Which always compels the holy way
to be on guard for viral menaces,
the thorn behind the gorgeous bloom,
is always seeking, exploiting
your fragile vessel of clay.

76. Beauty

Lord, beauty is the presence of you in us,
and we cannot live without it,
lest we become hardened, shortsighted, small.
Beauty is the scent we would emit
were we a gardenia,
it is the seed of perfection
trying to find its way to bloom,
the virtuous product of something
not made for mercenary pay,
not made for nominal passions,
but made so that we can
mirror you in a minor way,
by making something
"ever ancient, ever new."
    From Saint Augustine's *Confessions*

77. All Misinformed?

Lord Jesus, are we supposed to believe
that two millennia of believers
were all misinformed,
that your promise is a myth to deceive,
that those whose choice and Gregorian song
led them to monastic temperance,
that all those who chose you
in defiance of sure torture, were all wrong?

Are we supposed to believe
that those who could have avoided hungry leopards
in arenas and circuses,
who could have avoided peril
simply by recanting their belief in you,
were all misinformed?

Lord, the greatest testimonies of you,
are from the many who,
in the face of terror denied life itself
instead of denying you.
Help me have that courage
that is true of those who,
even against the might
and fright of Rome held onto
the promise you made at Calvary.

78. Deer Do Not Look Up

Lord, deer do not look up
but walk instead right under a hunter's stand,
never realizing the presence of danger.
The deer do not look up because
even though they are of you,
they have not been infused with your spirit,
and must think that there is nothing upward to see.

Some people do not look up
and instead, look forward
to their own pursuits,
blind like deer to your presence,
in danger, likewise.
O Lord, teach them vertical vision,
teach them that their lateral paths
are perilous. Amen.

79. Bring Back My Zeal

O Lord,
Bring back my zeal
in this almost spring,
when the sun's arc climbs,
the birds and trees on cue,
let me feel
the burst of soon growth bursts,
when the blue jay seeks and finds
his mate among the to-be buds.

I'm waiting now for hyper hope,
for effort-worthy work,
not the serial slope
of lost jumping juices
that slip with age.
O Lord, help me in my weakness,
should just doing be just enough,
without reward or glory,
help me with my could be fruits,
help me tell my story,
and I will seek your example, in meekness.

80. Eye vs. Mind

Father,
The mind discerns the sunrise
and the eye sees the light,
but only the heart, from your
invisible presence in it,
can feel and know wrong from right.

The mind thinks it knows,
but cannot always be trusted,
is often mistaken, and it shows.
The eye yearns to see
your grand design laid before it,
it seeks to mimic in its makings
its own paternity.

But the mind steps in,
and tries to take control,
it dictates, assumes authority,
but is blind to what the eye cannot see
which, in communion with the heart,
gives us substance, examples for our faith,
it gives us one of your oldest awards, Lord,
it gives us art.

81. Save Me Again

Father,
Racked by body spasm,
curled into a fetal coil
from injury, trauma, toil,
looking for release,
I writhe in bed and call
your name in prayer.
Bring back the sun,
cease the punishing rain,
lift me up and across
this time, this plight, this bed,
Lord, save me from the pain,
save me once again.

82. Our Choice

Lord,
Lingering pleasures in the tangling woo,
a choice between the daily diligent
evidence of a holy ghost, you,
or living day by day

with oneself as a lone pilot,
captain of sometimes merciless moments
when we are alone with our own way.

The choice seems clear,
either you or no you,
but we pray and you are near,
while others face the steady storms,
marooned with a dark wind over roiling water.

A choice is there, snakes and wasps
are gone after first hard frost,
all breathe an organic, in/out cycle
of new life, infant joy,
but we sing a prayer all around
for those loved, embraced, lost.

When our turn spins lickity split,
and we complete our cycle,
we've made our choice.
We are not alone and hear your voice
though not with ears,
that you are there for us for the asking,
and can and do assuage persistent fears.

We are all together in the tangling woo,
your laboratory for our possibilities,
should we or not heed your voice,
from gifts no other of your creatures have,
we believe this came from you, O Lord,
and we have made our choice.

83. Ex Members

Come to me,
O Lord,
and be my steward, shepherd,
captain of to-be passes,
I need you more than ever,
Lord,

I'm facing the cellular error,
Satan's seed planted within me
and within a plague on the masses.

I'm not the only one who lives
with biological terror,
I'm joining a club no one wants to join.
You're with us, Lord,
which ever way what happens happens,
you are with us when we wither
and with us when we prosper
and your cold wind snuffs the evil embers,
and we become contented,
released from the undesirable club,
ex members.

84. Either Here or There

Lord,
Either we are in your kingdom
or we are in a free-for-all,
with every man and woman for themselves,
making up rules as they go,
with rubber truth, elastic fact,
not knowing where we've gone wrong,
not seeing failed promises
that rot the root and vital stem,
not making a history call
and denying those things that have not worked
for the common good,
instead trying to resurrect them.

85. The Pretenders

Lord,
You are still in your reign,
in the other world as well as this,
now, after twenty centuries
it should be obvious to all
to not deny your grace.

You are the water for the thirsty,
desert rain, food for the hungry,
the arithmetic sum
of what has been all this time,
to where we have come,
past the dead corpses left by the godless,
in just the last hundred years, you win
and all the pretenders who do not know the peace
that comes from you, we pray for them,
O Lord. Amen.

86. Speck Seed

You set out from Zion, O Lord,
a speck, a cell on body earth,
you travelled to the limbs,
legs, arms, head,
planted your speck seed
that sprouted world over, first in Zion, then Rome,
then in all the other extremities
like a benevolent virus.

Your speck seed has spawned
generations of fishes and fishers,
spreading the way the rain does
when it falls here but ends up over there.
Many are in your lair,
and we pray for those who aren't.

87. Mother's Day

The wombs of our mothers
are the wellsprings of our waters.
Without them, our little oozings
would never grow into springs.
Before we knew the lighted space,
they were in our fetal dreams.

They carry us in situ and on shoulders,
give us blood and bone, exempt us from
an absence of love which smothers,

and are the center of the circle
that includes us, that includes our passage
from embryonic darkness into light.
Lord, thank you for our mothers.

88. The Unfound Thing and the Cheery Days

There is an ever present being-belly hunger all around
and should we ever gain access to all that we wish, from a list,
it would only be a matter of invisible time
until, after persistent volleys of joy rented
from things we say, insist
that would make us forever contented,
from roller coaster living
to cheesecake days we should soon discover
something missing from the list,
something we were not aware of in our cheery days,
something we had never found.

That unfound thing would be our undoing,
we would pine for it, eschewing
the cheery days, be peace resisting
and back to longing,
back to the median years
when we didn't know of its existing.

89. First and Last

Lord,
You suggested that for us to be first
we must be last,
so that we may succumb to humility.
You suggested that for us to be strong
we must be weak and meek
and thus inherit the earth.
You suggested that we consider the lilies
and toil not to be,
yet each year of our stay here
among the living
we encounter our slashings, passings,
as you did on Calvary.

We are all weak, Lord,
and a few of us accept it,
yet others do not and spend their days
trying to be first, best, strongest, fastest,
which leads to our fleshly progression
in the qualities of this one life
while at the same time can bring
a love of self which you eschewed.

Lord, those before and after you
said that should you be
who you said you were, then
you could have saved yourself on Calvary,
but you didn't because you had to show
that by being physically destroyed
beside two criminals
that you too could be last,
to die while others lived on,
but first to suffer while others witnessed,
first to verify what had been predicted,
first to show that by your living love cast,
you are first among mortals at any time,
any place, and that by dying, then returning,
there is reward for being last.

90. Approaching Zero

Father,
You take away the sins of the world,
have mercy on us,
you sometimes take away too
the good, the righteous
and leave the laggard, the weevils,
forcing us to ask if you are the justice maker
here, or only ever after.

You force us into doubt
in order for us to overcome it,
when we do we rejoice,
when we don't we have no choice

but to combust justice with a spark
of honor, but we do
such a poor job of it.

You force suspicion of what you render,
cause us to wonder why one was taken
who did as you asked,
while another who defied you
lived on, sometimes in splendor.

But what would there be need
for faith had faith not be needed,
all was predictable and we all knew what was to be?
We would all win the lottery,
we'd be untangled from not-knowing
but your grace we may not know
either, making all much less,
making all less sensible, indefensible,
approaching zero.

91. WE PLACE OUR BET

Father,
You have us suffer
and none of us gets through this life
without having to overcome something, but why?
We lose our loved ones, our health,
our wealth or hope,
we do not escape the trouble
before our time passes by.

We should know that none of us
will suffer as much as you
and by doing so we are closer to you
but better yet,
we grow stronger from our
weakened breaks
and we would surely have no humility,
no caution toward wrongdoing without

knowing that we are candidates for loss,
we place our bet
that we will endure and we will
with your grace.

92. Waiting for the Lilies

Lord, we're waiting for them to show themselves,
but they live in their own time
like the rest of us.
In some places they come back at Easter
like you did,
in other places, other times.

They have their buds now in March,
bullets ready to shoot
their colors for a short duration.
They come back from a winter death
and at such times we remember you
and how you did the same.

After their new life
they only show themselves for awhile,
like you did.
Lord, thank you for the lilies.

4

April

93. Bells of Rome

    Lord,
    I am across the night seas
    among umbrella pines and orange groves,
    atop one of seven hills far from home,
    the Aventine wind blows
    over your house of Santa Sabina,
    it is that time of day for prayer
    and I hear the bells of Rome.

I'm here where your spirit
still dwells in the brick and mortar,
where Peter, Paul, gentile and Jew
walked these hills,
I walk among the rubble too
of an empire, marble scattered
like litter, miles of brickwork,
ancient labors spent yet still seen,
the spring gives back its green
above all the hills and valleys below.

Your brothers built their massive domes,
hordes of people come to see and walk as I do,
among the shadows of time and story,
do they hear, as I do,
the bells of old Rome
calling them to you?

94. Your Breath

Lord,
Over the water above the blue
it's you, now,
I feel your breath
moving leaves, shifting sands,
filling sails, mussing hair
that falls gently over a brow
while I pray,
I feel your breath that snuffs a candle
but doesn't take the light
of the world away.

95. Small Castles

I trust in you, O Lord
for steerage.
I'm not asking for advantage
but only protection
from the jaws of circumstance.

Stay with me, Lord,
that I may survive to spend
another day that I may
do more to be worthy
of you, Lord.

I am in the foyer, Father,
waiting to know which door to take,
wanting the one that leads
to life, to make
small castles that could
contribute to something more than just
a whittler's passing of time in wood.

96. Your Gifts

I willingly receive your gifts, Lord,
of silhouetted evenings
along the freeway toward home.
The traffic swirls with commuters

hurriedly on their way somewhere
but over there, on the right,
is a forest where deer hide from headlights.

At home, the road is dark
and the rabbits are scurrying,
running across the road in flight.
I turn off my engine and hear an owl
hooting in hopes of hearing another.
Even without light your kingdom sings
in the dark, and I rejoice.

97. We Are Your Seeds and Chimes

Father,
We are the heirloom seeds
brought from other sproutings,
grown through two millennia.
We are the followers that bloom for you
in our given times,
regardless of the circumstances,
threats, maligned voices against us.

You are wind in weeds and woods,
now and in all times,
in the lake a white capping over blue,
in city streets, bustling steel belted speed living,
in the most remote wilderness
we are, and always will be
your ever ringing chimes.

98. Variation on the 23rd.

Lord,
You are my shepherd,
and I will never be in need.
I am led to restful waters by the lake
where the wind is free and is your breath.
You replenish my soul,
you lead me to where I am supposed to go,
and I go for your sake.
I fear no evil when I walk

the dark streets, for you are with me.
You anoint my head with unseen oil
that smells of olives and balsam,
and my cup of joy overflows.
With you, goodness and mercy
will follow me like a shadow cast from your light,
and I will dwell in your house forever.

99. When the Hammer Hits the Nail

Should we be in the winter of our years
and the skies fill with clouds, snow, wind, hail,
should we know you, Lord,
we will have no fear
when the hammer hits the nail.

Should we ever know that this day will be our last,
our hopes may fade, become weak, pale,
but should we know you our worries will be past,
when the hammer hits the nail.

Our duty is to love you, O Lord,
with all our maximum heart,
a test we should not fail
and should we love you,
our new life will just then start,
when the hammer hits the nail.

100. Mold

Lord, mold is the signature of death,
of darkness and inattention,
it corrupts the surface of anything shielded from light
and is a biological lie.

Mold is an unwanted fungus
of the living and soon to die,
Satan's green dust
that corrupts wood, leather, cloth, flesh,
the antithesis of illuminated trust.

Lord, if the opposite of you
had a badge, mold would be its mark,
it grows and grows willingly
but mostly in the dark.
It covers the bodies of the shadow stricken,
the unloved, the forgotten, sorrow spent,
and except in cheese
leaves its unwanted, pungent scent.

101. Receiving Her Peace

Lord,
She's wandering the halls now
searching for herself,
inching her way toward the century mark.
She doesn't remember the wagon and mule days,
old black cars with spoked wheels,
her cousins going off to fight the Nazis,
big burgers on big buns Sundays,
her Texas peaches out the windows,
carports with cats,
her hero beside her in a recliner.
Her years have become a thief,
her days a punishment.
One day when peaches are growing or not,
may be summer and if so, hot,
she will receive her peace and final place
with you, O Lord.

102. The Pass

Father,
I will strengthen my drooping hands
and make straight the paths of my feet,
because you do discipline us
and scourge your sons.

I will take my scarring as a seal
that you do not give
your believers a pass

from the heartaches of all their brothers and sisters,
else deniers would embrace you
only for the pass.
    From Hebrews 12:12, 13

103. A Bundle

Here I am, Lord,
worth nothing for my pounds of flesh
while rib eyes sell for exalted prices,
and without community
cannot compete in the tangled, mangled
forest of a day's jungle,
I'm left to my own devices,
ones you gave me,
and you gave me a bundle.

I cannot run like a cat,
fly like a hawk or supersonic bat,
detect a piece of bread in a child's hand
a mile away like a seagull,
swim like an otter,
climb like a squirrel,
have strength like a gorilla, grizzly or bull,
all I have is what you gave me,
while thrown into a pit
with steep walls that need climbing,
and what I have done with the bundle.

104. The Sacred or the Profane

Lord,
The choice is between
the sacred or the profane,
we can accept something
beyond humanity in your name
or we can continue doing
what we have been doing,
as we go along our tragic way
and be like the news accounts

of the transgressions we see
against our fellow man every day.
Lord, please help us embrace the former.

105. Choose Life

Father,
Mostly they fight the black dragon of death,
struggling with him when he comes,
showing up one day with a hungry lump in a chest or breast.
Mostly they choose life and resist
any effort to take it away at any time,
but she submits, giving in to what others cherish.
She weeps for what once was,
sitting, laying alone in her nursing home
which smells of elderly hostages of time,
hiding in sleep hours of the day,
waiting for the inevitable which she wishes would come,
waiting for the end, for that moment
when she will be released from wanting,
waiting for when she no longer
has only her memory that doesn't comfort her,
a memory that fuels her condition,
that includes visitors on Sundays after church
and years of working beside her life's companion,
which makes me wonder at what point,
if ever, will I follow and resign,
and let go of that which you have given.
I pray, never.

106. The Buoyancy of Your Ways

Lord,
Let me drift on blue yonder water,
float on a current of days,
with the banks as pleasing
as those already passed,
let me swim the cool eddies
and be carried over deep pools
by the buoyancy of your ways
O Lord.

107. New Arising

Lord,
Rain and not rain,
the fish are joy-swimming
at the new arising,
their bouillabaisse blood anxious.
The wasps are looking for a home,
soon, if not now, water moccasins
will be out looking for other moccasins,
the armadillos are already out
doing their damage, like cats to a yard,
they dig holes as aggravating
as feline claws on carpet.

Whiteout rain comes in,
the sun now spent,
the fish sleep with open eye,
wasps hide under an azalea crimson tent,
keeping their papery wings dry.

Thunder gives the early owls
some of their own medicine,
the coyotes are awakening
and stretching their throats in warm up.
I sit back like a voyeur, sneaking peeks,
at lightening flashes or a camera,
everything is looking for something
or someone,
crappies are in the shallows,
a hawk is raising cane,
crawfish dream of land
where they can crawl about and be versatile
as visitors from water
while risking hawk beak attacks.

We appreciate, marvel, pause.
April is beaming bounties progressively greening,
waters not yet now receding, the sun reasserting
its kingdom, as it ever was,
we acknowledge a new arising and we know its cause.

108. By the Spoonful, Every Hour, Every Day

Lord,
Your enemies are many,
they ally themselves in multitudes
and are arrayed like Solomon in their wealth,
in their power and armaments
against your sanctity.

They mock you and ignore you
as well as that day when their own lives
will end without hope.
They make all manner of efforts
to suppress the sacred,
hang salvation with a human rope,
and in the sacred's place a space
for those like themselves,
give each other celebrated awards,
rewards, commendations for work done their way,
approving, promoting, selling death
by the spoonful, every hour, every day.

Lord, I pray for them
and ask that you not allow
my anger to be riled by their guile.

109. Walking Horizontally

Here it comes, Lord,
another flight of stairs.
It's been so easy walking horizontally,
watching wind make water dance,
hearing a mid morning murder
of hysterical crows carry on,
hearing the music of the woods,
still believing we all have a chance
to walk horizontally again
with you as our shadow.

110. We, And the Tulip

Lord,
You came here to help us cope
with breakings beyond repair,
not to always prevent them because
you set in motion free will
among the weeds, and wishes of men,
spontaneous radial expansions,
not predictable ones, so
that we may know fear.

You gave us an opportunity,
an ability to overcome, to love,
morn, forgive, grow,
how sadly does the tulip slow
and give up its brief medallion shaped color.

We are here and you are in us,
part of us as surely as is the buzzard to his dingy wing,
the frog to his elastic tongue, bass to golden roe,
we, and the tulip know
we cannot be here forever.

Calamities claim their clients
like the sea that regurgitates its trash
and washes it ashore
and we are always shocked
and hope that we are not among them,
yet we, and the tulip carry on,
regrowing our way evermore,
through peril, joy and faith
in you, O Lord,
or else we perish in hopeless tides.

111. Bring Back the Sun

Lord,
Are those Van Gogh's crows overhead,
is that your tap at my door I hear?
Will I rise again above the devious dangers,

will the sun be doused with rain?
I'm ready if you are, Lord,
its not the end but the pain
that often accompanies it I fear.

My bags are packed, Lord,
for whenever the terminal taxi honks,
demons have slain the angels,
the Rome of our hearts has been sacked.
Please, Lord, keep me here
to finish my developing task,
allow me to finish what I've begun,
bring back beauty that was there,
before your enemies shunned it,
bring back the sun.

112. Caterwauling

Feline cries, moonlight moans,
in the woods of no help or hope,
lost in catness, in pursuit
of nothing but the night.

She moans and calls for others,
for feline rescuers, begging in dark sweetgums,
competing with wiley coons,
slow minded possums,
and coyotes that would make her into supper.

She's like the rest of us
among the helpless, Lord,
who need you every day
or know those who do.

113. Hitting Homers for the Devil

St. Paul said knowledge inflates with pride,
but love builds up,
and I say yes, Lord,
your servant, your fullback,

partaker of your bread, wine,
who carries the ball across the goal line,
or wins the game in overtime.

Yes, love builds up in degrees,
in groups, communities, cities, nations,
whenever it is promoted
by those sure of your stations,
that you did and are
what you say you are
but, sorrowfully, with us some are always in denial,
and some always at war.

The peacemakers are on your side, Lord,
we are the meek,
but those who believe in you, in love, peace, charity,
have to defend ourselves
against any and all who seek
to diminish you as they always have,
or who take violence as an offense,
throwing touchdowns,
hitting homers for the devil.
Amen.
   From 1 Corinthians 8:1

114. Without Pain

Lord,
Let me be rubber bodied
and bounce back bucking consequence
from assaults of viral, bacterial and pollen invaders,
seditious warriors against flesh and bone.

Let me be in remission of sin
and sorrow, malignant, irregular
sectors, squatters within,
free from cellular ruin under the skin,
bone breaks, unsolicited schisms of peace,
in order to love you
without pain.

115. Eternal Life

Your promise is the default spirit,
O Lord,
and for those who turn the other way from you,
all ends in terminal dirt,
the same fecund earth where joyous seed
with its internal instructions to grow and bloom,
its DNA endowed blueprint,
is ruptured of its inertia
and for those not listening, their passing
is a gloomy day indeed.

If for no other reason than
the cold finality of the opposite
without you, O Lord,
what reason is there to carry on,
to build our houses on sand?
The alternative without you is permanent death,
and with you, eternal life.

116. And the Rain Comes Down

Each drop is a footstep
and the rain comes down.
Each drop is a doorstep,
common as October yellowing leaves,
your fingerprint on every one,
O Lord,
evidence of your order in the oaks and pines.

The flux of seasons indicates motion
put in action by something
because there is no movement without force
like the inevitables captained by your spark
that's there in every sphere,
you are in the leaf and every water drop on it
here and near,
and the rain comes down.

117. Tired Arms

Lord,
Don't let my arms get tired
like Moses' in the battle at Rephidim,
let them be strong
like your arms on the cross.

Save me from that fatigue that comes
from frail epitomes of weakened
brothers and sisters,
from struggles with disappointment
that others do not see your strength,
your arms nailed in place,
never tiring.
   From Exodus 17:12

118. Cycles

He lays there asleep
in his bed like a fallen cherub,
has survived infancy, the throes
of traversed toddlerhood, and now, at six
awaits a boyhood of action figures,
cowboys, monsters, heroes.

He will continue his cycle into
young manhood, not understanding his changes,
discover girls, love, heartbreak,
and evolve into a man
with a beard that, over time,
becomes gray along with his hair
and will find himself there
at a place where he already is
whatever he will be
and must accept either you, Lord,
or lose his chance at eternity.
For Kincaid, 2010

119. Your Bounties

Lord,
You gave us hope,
luminous light, mystique of night,
mystery of you, heart beating,
vascular vouchers, charity, faith.

You are the liver giver,
the organ donor who donates all,
pushing muddy river currents, revolving seasons
that keep our years diverse,
protect us from the worst of our maladies,
we are what we are because of your gifts.
Lord, thank you for your bounties.

120. I'm Here

Lord Jesus,
I've had to walk a straight line
with a crooked foot,
had to see your ribbon light
through boney woods
but with a crooked eye too,
had to watch and wait, here,
where I see with monocular sight,
but what am I yet,
but what I've not been given by you?
I could have been a windshield bug,
a rodent eaten by a quick cat
in some soggy forest,
could have been a bat
feeling my way,
a slug slung into salty seas,
could have been a mule,
a four legged eunuch eating hay, too,
whose time has come and gone,
an eagle who was almost gone but came back,
could have been a whale in an infinity of blue,
but instead, I'm here, where I hear
June bugs batting at my front door,
even in early April.

121. I Hear Cecelia Singing

I hear Cecelia singing,
singing for the rain that soothes
the hopes of weeping leaves, starving trees,
singing for the hopeless souls
trapped within their sulfurous sufferings,
singing for a faith that cannot
be removed through force or fear,
for the imprisoned, persecuted,
ridiculed, ignored or subjugated
because of you, O Lord,
singing for the light that through
her cruel cage never seeped,
for her beacon of courage
that has not died in eighteen centuries,
that shows us even now
how we can use and be used by you, O Lord,
the way you intended.

122. Heartcentric

Lord,
In most of your creatures
the heart is merely a pump,
a turbine for venal combustion,
delivery engine of red liquid,
but in us, your pride and joy
it can be more than a nose is to a raccoon,
more than running speed to a savanna cat,
more than just a survival implement,
sonar for a black night bat,
more than just an internal space taker
but instead, one that thinks as it pumps
with a mind that feels,
living in you, O Lord.

5

May

123. We Should Listen to What's Been Said

Tolerance of evil is not a virtue,
and justice delivered to it no vice.
We should indeed turn our other cheeks,
but should not submit to tyranny
or butter the devil's bread,
we should know what has been done,
what some have done and can do,
we should listen to what's been said,
O Lord, by you.

Should we be pushed
we should first decline,
but then push back,
we should not dine with cannibals,
dance with serpents,
walk with demons,
allow sin to spawn, instead,
we should know what we can do
and listen to what's been said,
O Lord, by you.

124. Holy Certification

Lord,
Implanted in even the wicked
is the seed planted by your Father
that knows yet sometimes denies

right and wrong,
that defies Satan's pledge,
seeks, renders, plies
to end the world of righteousness
you consecrated, Lord,
you verified, fertilized the seed
that sprouts in tears and joys,
your pedigree of love
that never dies through millennia
where many labors have been spent
in praise, in art, architecture,
in marble saints and musty churches
where we still bow in thanks
for your holy certification.

125. Lead Me to My Call

Lord,
Many have given their all,
martyrs, monks, preachers, priests,
missionaries, deacons, and nuns
have followed you and surrendered
themselves not just to you
but to be in you.

Many have sacrificed
a one and only physical life
for your promise of a better,
a precious gamble,
have been burned, beheaded, scourged,
and proven their faith
and thus are, as a body,
the greatest evidence of your spirit.

Lord, my misfortunes are small,
I'm embracing all
of your holy plentitudes,
I've yet to suffer a scar
in championing you, Father.
Lead me to my call.

126. Work

Lord,
We are stranded here,
and in these cellular structures we are many,
marching forward in mandatory steps,
surrounded by a sleeping
and sometimes waking fear.

We have benefitted from your loss,
when you defied the existing powers,
and threw their might back at them,
now, your strength is ours,
garnished your strength, your love, your cross.

We are put here for a test, a quiz,
with a purpose, a reason,
and our duty is to forever search,
find out what it is,
ours is always the searching season.

We are here to work,
for "he who does not work, neither shall he eat,"
yet we provide for those unable
to do their walking with their feet,
the sick, the crippled, the weak,
just as you did
so, in faith, should we have it
we show it
and that is part of our purpose,
our work, should we just know it.
      From: Thessalonians 3:10

127. The Restraining Effect

Lord,
What would the world be bereft,
should we be left
without the restraining effect
you have on all of us,

on communities where lust
for all favors hides
within the human breast?

Should we be absent
of the doctrinal love and peace
you propose,
by the authority you have
that backs up what is right,
and scorn for wrongdoing, I suppose
the ever present but sometimes subdued
beast within the heart of man
would be unleashed
and feel no dissuading
to launch the dark one's carnal command.

128. Waiting Simply

Father,
We feel the razor's blade in these lives,
we lose our limbs, ears, eyes,
our lovers, mothers, others.

When young we turn cartwheels across the floor,
when old we can barely walk across it.
She took the final step toward you
and now her chair beside me is empty.

We get, we give and wait simply
to take our place, knowing that our ancestors
are grave bound in their flesh like cicada shells
left on trees and collected by children.

129. Be With Me Lord

When misery visits the temple of the body,
when muscles, bones, vessels and such
bring pain and I seek relief,
be with me Lord, when I am in trouble.

When tragedies arrive and they always do,
for even the richest of us can be poor in spirit,
when loved ones suffer, their miseries double
and we all sit at the table of the misbegotten,
when your bright light of the sun is gone,
the warmth passed, trees bare, the flowers rotten,
be with me Lord, when I am in trouble.

When our families or friends are in danger,
so too are we,
waiting with a prayer, a request, a plea,
for your loving mercy to descend on us,
on them, on me,
be with me Lord, when I am in trouble.

130. Walking in Shadow

Lord,
I have walked along in shadow,
in search of what is right
among shade trees
in avoidance of a searing sun,
along a river that runs into years,
in hunger and as St. Augustine said,
restless until I rest in Thee,
searching, hoping to come out of the shade
and into the light
that is you, O Lord.
      From: *The Confessions of Saint Augustine*

131. Cattle Egrets

Cattle egrets follow the heifers
over just rained on fields,
where the patties have been
softened by the weather,
they come behind the hooves,
beak searching for insects
disturbed by sloven, cloven Brahma beeves,
sometimes they ride on the backs

of indifferent, monstrous bulls,
doing what matadors wished they could do
in their Minoan fresco dreams,
and manage to stay snowy white
amidst scented brown droppings surrounding them.
They are the ornaments, Lord,
on your greeny, greeny tree of life.

132. The Theft

Lord, you took her away from me
without notice,
and I felt her body warmth leave
right at my fingertips
and fly away like a night bird.

You stole her spark
the way a rain takes a fire
and left her flesh,
and I held her cold hands
as her spirit fled.

All my days had always had her in them.
She bought my first cowboy hat,
she brought my first love,
and in her absence I mourn
and wait to join her in your house
after my own fire is ash.

133. You Lend Your Hand

Lord,
You lend your hand,
with our handless and handy
and to the comfortable too
who are still uncomfortable without you,
with those who seek
and those who don't for help,
your indecipherable needed net is there
for all those who weep.

You lend your hand
in the tidy and jumbled order of substance,
in the irrepressible march of surely spring,
or ice, whale births at sea, volcano, water, land,
you are the heartbeat of the pulsing,
gravity embracing tug of this,
primordial schematic of what exists,
and what does not.

You lend your hand
in weeping willows and pillows,
where we sleep and sometimes see you,
in lantanas that grow like fire ant mounds,
in the lung that breathes
a sigh of life,
in the sun's morning, day's demise,
moon shadow, early dew.

134. Puppy Road

She always loved dogs,
and said she'd never seen an ugly one.
She talked often of her beloved dachshund
and how he saved her from solitude.

On the way to her funeral,
on a road traveled over and over,
there where the road straightens
was a puppy, reminding me of her.

Lord, was this your way to speak,
that you knew my grief?
Was this your unexpected sign,
not spoken in any language
except one of faith
that somehow you would reach me?

From experience I know
that you provide the beak that breaks the shell,
your moon persuades the tides,
you rattle the reeds
just enough for those who are listening,
not with their native ears
but watchful, nonetheless,
just enough for receptive hearts,
just enough to tell.

135. Our Enemies

Lord,
We are standing face to face now
with an enemy who thinks we are evil.
Please ease this confrontation.
Our brothers are armed though with more than swords.
Our enemies disavow us and you
and wish for our humiliation.
They wait with death planned for our demise.
Is this your way of telling us that we have all disappointed you?
Is this your way of telling us we are near an end?
Please deliver us from all this conflict and potential loss.
Please hear our prayers and allow for conciliation.
Amen

136. Swallowed Up In Victory

Lord,
We are the firstfruits of your creatures,
you have freed our feet from stumbling,
have heard our voices in supplication,
you set the captives of cold hearts free,
you thwart the wicked either now or later,
you are the bread that came down from heaven,
we can feel you, know you, but not see
and have to replace doubt with care,
worship at your footstool,
and wear you as a garment,
so death will be swallowed up in victory.
>From: I Corinthians 15:5

137. If You Allow It

Lord,
I'll take a hoe and clear
a line of weeds
that grow more readily
than the vegetables.
I know you are near.
I'm asking for your help
with some of my urgent needs,
that my spouse will outlive me,
that my children will always be free
from ugly power
and those who abuse it.

I'll continue to stumble and recover
if you allow it.
I don't expect a life without challenge,
without loss, the way weeds grow willingly,
without encouragement,
and I'll discover
ways to grow in spite of them,
if you allow it, Lord.

138. Death by Ice

Here in the ever quivering fluid
of your eternal dynamics, O Lord,
we live and breathe a finite life
like your creations, all,
we bud and bloom, learn to speak and sing,
shiver in cold and wait for spring,
wallow in the bounties of summer
and remember what once was in the fall.

O Glorious life that you afford,
given to us as a proving ground
by you to see how we perform,
either basking in your grace
or living with our own accord
we go,

but whatever choice we make,
should we take our chips, roll the dice,
like the lily that should remind us of you,
O Lord,
we face in winter death by ice.

139. That Still Branches Today

Lord,
They came home triumphant from Jerusalem,
building Titus' arch
with stone Roman soldiers
marching with high stepping horses.
Little did they know
that in victory they sealed their own defeat,
when your followers in the Eternal City
died for you with seditious passions
in arenas and coliseums,
their blood was the food of your vine,
that still branches today.

140. Thank You for Both

Heavenly Father,
Dia, Dios, Deus, God of all,
help me in my journey
towards you,
let me see how far I can go,
only you know
what will bear.

Thank you for another day,
each is a present
opened at dawn,
another say, play,
stay, way with you.

Thank you for this one
with her,
mother of your presents,

spouse and always companion
through all the days.
Thank you for both.

141. Organic Currency

Lord Jesus,
Your woven fabric at night
gives gray moonlit branches growing
in places where branches can only grow,
interlaced, moving into available space,
such tapestry, what a travesty
to ignore its author.

You make a thread
and take its head
into living circuitry,
organic currency,
while we all dance to your music,
whether we know it or not.

142. Never Not Showing Up

Lord, the Psalmist was right,
you wrap yourself in light as with a garment
and stretch out the heavens like a tent too.
You play hide and seek with us
every day, every hour,
catch me if you can behind a shadow,
pouring rain or gentle shower,
you sometimes reveal yourself to us
but are always camouflaged,
hidden like your own feathered grouse,
your leaf imitating caterpillars,
copperheads and owls.

But you were always there since time began,
in light, word and love, never not showing up,
we've drunk from your many flavored cup,
we'll take you any way we can.

If some may suspect your absence
in war, sickness, feckless fate,
it is us who have not shown up
with resistance to those who
create so much woe.
Stand up, stand up, my fellows
and don't blame our Lord
for our own misdeeds
which, through our ambivalence
to our own sons and daughters we bestow.
   From: Psalms 104:2

143. Thankful

Thankful for the blessed life I seek,
that I have been given, O Lord,
one not absent but short on sorrow,
to look up at the evening sky,
with rain falling in my face,
falling on my cheek, my eye
that sees the glimmer of the day's shadow,
the sky opaque, sun dimming,
of color fading into the west
and into tomorrow.

144. For the Making of Better Others

Lord,
The sun yellows the green, green grasses,
the light collapses at dusk
but she shines regardless,
spelunker like light breaking,
precious, uniquely yours
and of your making,
she's become an echo in a mirror,
a watchdog from old and older times,
knows who knows and who's faking,
solid, statuesque pattern producer,
the prototype mold
for the making of better others.

145. My Living Days

Lord Jesus,
Forgive me of my sour sins
which keep creeping, year by year,
up on me, hiding in absentia
to spring open and corrode
a faith that needs tending,
that must forever need a listening ear,
in order to faintly hear
the messages you keep sending.

Help me keep an open eye
that sees the miracles of your ways,
marshaled all about me,
on earth, sea, and sky.
Help me keep my footing
with my moorings tied to you,
in all my living days.

146. In the Land of *Before I Knew*

Once, in the land of *Before I Knew*,
I could call my mother on the phone,
speak to her, hear her laugh,
visit her and eat her chicken and dressing,
before I knew she would be taken from me.

When I lived in the land of *Before I Knew*,
I could walk the fields with my grandfather,
on our way to feed his cows I could hear
his rubber boots sloshing in the mud,
before I know he would one day be gone.

When I lived in the land of *Before I Knew*,
I had no grandchildren,
no little grandson imitating heroes,
no granddaughter with baby dolls and dresses,
now I know and they are blessed.

Am I still living in the land of *Before I Knew?*
Is there something that I don't know,
that one day will just show up,
and be grand, or ghastly?
Lord, I'm leaving that up to you.

147. No Other Choice

Lord,
There is no other choice but you.
We have seen the alternatives,
and have seen what they can do.
We know them by their fruits,
a trail of recent blood,
their greedy soil defaulted, salted,
and we know now that you were right
in saying the exalted shall be humbled,
and the humbled exalted.
From Matthew 23:12

148. These Are The Days

Lord,
It is a conversation with myself and you.
The blackbirds are cackling, making their noise,
doves gather, rest on limbs and coo,
there are dances in the branches
with your almighty hand that moves the leaves and waves,
a perfection issues forth, an Inness gold to behold,
as it always does when the light is low,
especially in San Antonio.
You are there
and I know it is you who saves.

These are the days
when being amongst the living
makes us aware, should we pause to know
your eternal giving of the little candies
sometimes so easily ignored.
These are the fruits of the be-tree,

the be-me, cognizant of your
old oak acorns to be stored,
ever free for the taking, your jubilant cause,
my dog at my side, awakening,
your furry gift to humanity.

These are the days so simply here,
day dying, evening ensuing,
the days we will remember
when all is alive, including us,
and you are near.

149. Wiltings

In the summer of our day the light casts strong shadows
but then begins to wilt like a flashlight near its end.
The water holds the light
like a low battery losing its charge
when the dusk ensues and between the black trees
there is a wilting blue above red,
the blue too blackens, the red wilts to orange, then crimson
which wilts to violet, then black when the winter of our day
is upon us and the color has been bled from the sky.

The night too wilts in early woods,
along interstates truckers welcome it,
it seeps upon us like an odor
of slowly cut garlic in a small room,
like a truth that spreads among liars,
an incremental light providing its silent particle motor.
We open our eyes and it is ours.

150. Expand the Hours

She's my co-breath beside me
in the winter when muddy clouds puddle
and the cold wind is breezing past the door,
she is covered up in quilts
and likes to cuddle.

In the middle of the night I wake
and hear her breathing, then
know that I am alive
for you have given me an echo
of myself beside me, to take
forever as my own.

In the summer when the ceiling fans
are moving the air around like weightless sheep,
she lays beside me in quiet sleep,
in dreams without duties,
without fears, worries, demands.

In the spring she bends to plant the flowers,
moments we all wish we could freeze,
she's got her herbs and azaleas too,
they burst in brilliant color with much ado,
O Lord, how I wish we could forever
expand the days, the blooms, the hours.

151. He Strives To Be

Lord Jesus,
The big moon's over Mississippi,
it's over here too, pale day in night to see,
I'm looking up at it,
thinking of him, his day old heart hurting,
pee-wee lungs struggling,
on this May night he strives to be.

While on this same date
others never even reach his short step,
never see mother-father faces,
he rushes uphill, the moon rises,
shines on his neonatal crisis,
others worry, tied in knots
at what is or worse, some ugly fact,
on this illuminated night with dirty light,
windless trees, weak shadows,
he strives to be.

All goes on as if
he were or weren't in it,
he's yet to set his fit.
While others less deserving die of old age
or calcify in nursing homes,
wishing they didn't have
what we wish he did.

In the river current, tidal wash of moonlit sea,
amongst the living, breathing,
on only his second day among us,
his jeopardy shows us all
the simple oxygen privilege,
cardiac music, percussive assurance,
the internal body dance that we endure,
enjoy, engage, our organic pedigree,
our normal nomenclature,
while he strives to be.

152. Dreaming While Awake

Lord, I'm dreaming while awake
when the rain descends,
it waters the thirsty grasses,
pours, puddles, soaks.
I'm dreaming of a day
when we'll all be eating
golden acorns from golden oaks,
when weightless bodies will be our gifts,
when we will be the lost ones found,
our hearts at rest, not beating,
when, light as fireflies
we will need our own combustion for fuel
to further us no more,
but will circle like electrons
around your holy, sparking core.

We'll float like Luna moths
around bright light sources,
content in what we are,
desiring not, our lives having
run their courses,
and will sing in chorus
with celestial choirs
when we are taken up by you
after our final farewell hours.

No longer struggling with gravity,
with day to day torque,
we have found the right road,
taken the right fork
that leads to you, O Lord.

153. LA LUZ DE DIOS

Holy Father,
Your light enters my eye
and bounces back into paint
then reflects again to another
and gives reason to take up space,
revisit it and hand it back
as an offering, a painting,
a child of the color of grace.

6

June

154. Provide the Ways

Heavenly Father, the days go by drudgingly without her,
mornings without calls, evenings without contact.
I still hear her voice beckoning me,
reaching out through my childhood,
through adolescence, mid-life,
and now, the stillness of silent mornings,
empty nights, keeps reminding me
of what she gave.

Lord, provide the ways
with ample reason to carry on,
to replenish zeal, brand new baby making joy,
that spills over days by days
and lets us continue with losses,
that we had always dreaded.

155. Disorderly Order

Lord, I've noticed that among the lakeshore weeds
that grow without persuasion or acceptance,
there is structure as if spaghetti
had been neatly arranged like ordered fodder,
symmetry among asymmetry, a tapestry of woven greens
on a loom of light and water.

At a distance the weeds are an undesirable mass,
taking up space, attempting hegemony
with their green, ubiquitous armies, nature's faces,
but up close they are refined, sleek,
orangey-stained, ordered in their slender spaces.

I've noticed too a botanical understanding,
a zoological knowledge that,
for instance, there is seldom a snake
among the brushes and marshes of the lake
because the herons seek them out, catch them,
and whip their own long necks like cowboy ropes
until the snakes themselves are ropes,
lifeless, without coil,
at which time the heron has his breakfast,
feasting on a serving of immaculate design.

156. My Germ

Father,
What do you have in store for me?
I know that I am only
a body among many,
a grain of corn among fields,
yet I also know that each grain
has a germ ready to rise into new life,
a green rocket planted by you.

Lord,
Secure my germ, let it flourish,
protect me from the fires of wrath
the way you protected Saint Polycarp,
guide me in my path,
keep me in your way
until my time is done.
Amen.

157. Once Again Serving

Lord, thank you for allowing me to stop
two box turtle's lengths away
from a dangerous leaf hidden snake,
my exposed ankle amply available.
I could just as well
have been the captain of the Titanic,
Darius at Guagamela, or Lee at Gettysburg,
making a wrong turn on a field or sea,
but I stepped with horizontal gravity,
and you were once again serving,
showing your grace,
saving me once again,
and am I so deserving?

158. The Cleansing

Father of all,
the cleansing comes
and we know from where,
it drips from thirsting leaves,
the roots of trees rejoice
and we know that you are there.

The cleansing refutes heat,
soothes the barren lung,
we hear its dripping cadence,
we feel its soothing presence
and know that you have sung.

The cleansing tiptoes silently
on the hot metal roof that steams,
it's part of the parcel
of your gift to all given,
replenishes earth, fields, rivers, streams.

159. On My Way

On my way to 365,
how do I love thee, O Lord,
let me pray the ways,
let me wake each day
to the end of the year,
hear your soft voice
of wind in my ear,
see your golden light touch
the curtain by the window
that shines and shows
the woods outside still
verdant, fervent in its march
of the living, the running,
the flying, growing, hiding,
swimming, breathing world
that you and no other, have made.

160. The Choice

Lord,
You could have given us no choice
in Eden or even now, instead,
the way of the dumb creatures
of the earth who cannot discern tomorrow,
you could have had us helpless,
foraging for our food
at the mercy of chance as some still do,
with no preparation of consciousness,
but you didn't.
You gave us the chance to discern,
succeed or fail, and some of us, all of us
do sometimes fail,
yet ours is the prerogative to decide,
ours is a choice,
all but for the many left behind
of what kind of ride
we will take through miles of ages.

161. Almost Forever

A sieve sifts all, Lord,
except rocks which last almost forever,
but all else is pounded into pebble,
memory dust of us and our labors
extends itself well past these moments.

The work that we mostly do
in sweetness or shards found
by archaeologists with hard hats,
hard routine, our efforts spent to fill
our quota enough to deny a vacuum
with dead days, unloved hammer hours,
some bona fide, rarefied ones,
of traffic hum, honkings on, sirens in night skies,
air itself sieved and served
after a Saturday sundown that seemed
to last almost forever.

162. Whatever It Is

The clock moves on
closer to my goal,
days, nights are massing,
loves, lives, times are passing
but I'm not ready yet,
O Lord,
my plans from you are not yet set,
at least I hope not now,
I'm waiting to see, to find
what you want from me,
what you have in store for thine.

Whatever it is, Lord,
I've learned from my brethren, my kin,
from what I've heard
the righteous life rewards itself,
again and again,
one of truth in you that replenishes the aural spin,

shuns self adornment, hubris in the suburbs,
one that knows the grace of you, Lord,
one that disparages ruinous sin.

163. Tis the Digging That is Good

Were it not for digging holes,
finding no gold rocks, only bones,
partials in pale content,
should I find them they may
make me something other if I would
but should know from you,
tis the digging that is good.

We are ready with hands, body,
substance built for shovels
to uncover unwanted soil,
lies old as humus, rotten dirt,
my co-self beside me,
both of us digging our way
through weedy, woodsy bramble
that has to be restrained, and we should,
lest it be a contagion blinding,
not allowing us to see,
tis only the digging that is good.

164. One Eye

Lord,
You took away one of my eyes
so I could see you better,
so let me go on seeing more with less.
Let me listen for less than Elijah's wind
as it wisps quietly past my ear
like a silk scarf swimming in a breeze.
Let me remember how to hear your wind
as a breath that rustles the dust on back roads,
and moves the trees and grasses to dances.
Let me look for you in your subtle stances,
at the edge of sight,

out of the corner of my one eye,
your stealth presence only slightly
seen in glances.

165. Mustard Seed

I am the mustard seed
that sprouted in the soil,
O Lord,
you cleanse my spirit,
you anoint my soul in oil
and I will not lose it
but let in grow in the sun
with all my faith
in the father, spirit and son.

166. Googling Heaven

Lord God Almighty,
I Googled heaven
and it fell into my lap,
strait from the stars
from the bottomless top.

Now I know from digital fact that she
will spend Christmas somewhere else,
detached from mortals
the way a leaf detaches from a tree.
Green leaves never grieve
for their fallen orange brothers
the way we grieve for mothers,
brothers, sisters, lovers.

I shuffle now without a shadow
following me like a rumor.
The shuffle is quiet without audience,
talk, plans, encounters.
When I shuffled then I knew what history was.
I danced with music of the ages
sent from buggy days and kerosene lamp nights.
I danced with her.

167. The Notion of Liberty

Lord,
You said that they will know us
by our fruits
and yes, of those not just now
or yesterday but over the ages.

Those who have followed you
have had more prosperity,
liberty, justice, longevity,
than those who have not.

There has been a discernable providence,
and many rewards others never see
to those who believe
that love of you brings goodness
to those who know
that there is holiness in the notion of liberty.

168. More Prosperous Than All the Rest

Heavenly Father,
Some are born with beauty
which time steals away,
some with wealth
which someone else takes from them,
some are born with nothing
but yet are beautiful to you,
and are rich if they follow you
having that which money cannot buy
and beauty not impress,
those who have you are
more prosperous than all the rest.

169. A Life Bestowed

The child leaps and laughs,
he runs and romps and plays,
imagines dragons, giants, heroes,
and his innocence is sure as skin.

The adolescent grows and knows
he has a dragon in his chest,
he loves with love's extremes,
but does not know what love is,
but knows that it is his.

At maturity he sets his cleats
to make his run,
sprints through days,
his day's duties seldom done.

Then, older, he's got a catalogue of faces,
ones he knew, abhorred, adored, loved,
he's made his mark,
run his races.

At old age all he's got
is what he remembers,
his fire fueled with gray embers,
a life bestowed upon him
by you, O Lord.

170. Thank You for the Music

Lord,
You gave us strings
that sound like our souls,
you gave us horns
that sound like our voice,
percussions that sound
like our hearts.

You gave us guitars,
those repositories of finger feelings,
you gave us pianos
that sound like our thoughts,
solos, symphonies, combos,
so that music is the crow-call
of all of us.
Lord, thank you for the music.

171. Duty

Lord,
We are not here to just relax or coast,
not here to envy, hate,
deceive, covet or boast.
We are not here for inaction
while others provide our bread,
not here just for carnal pleasure,
for epicurean indulgence,
nor to judge our fellow man,
but here, instead,
to contribute to the human pie,
for even the simplest of labors
provides a benefit to others,
so all may feel a part
of the community of those
who lend a hand.

172. Fireflies Sparkle

Fireflies sparkle like twinkling stars
when night becomes to day a moat,
there is owl-hoot in the holler,
a frog croaks somewhere
like someone clearing his throat.

Fireflies sparkle away from city lights,
in backyards where the urban glow
is muffled in the night, they are tiny candles,
their chemical luminescence dancing in their flights.

They are your little beacons blinking
above blanket black skies, Lord,
I was on my porch and thinking.
I watched the sparkles as they flew
and thought, Lord, are these your eyes?

Fireflies sparkle, have they ever so?
In streets where the night has been subdued
they are the candies of a darkened sight,
little flying embers in the night.

173. Ante Over

    When I play ante over with you,
    Lord, I will know that you're
    on the other side, waiting.
    I'll be the ball and I'm not concerned
    that you won't receive me,
    I'm anticipating,
    hoping, praying, that you will catch me
    with the palm of your hand.
    I will depart from chains of gravity then,
    will fly, leave this land
    with the milk of ages in my mouth,
    the light of golden beams in my eye,
    with angels accompanying me in my flight,
    transcending rooftops, levitating over and away
    and it will be a wondrous night,
    or a glorious day,
    O Lord.

174. Your Ants

    Your ants crawl over the earth,
    make mounds, nests, cities,
    their DNA launches them into uniqueness
    and there across yards
    or over urban freeways they go,
    to and from here and there
    living out their lives in motion,
    always going somewhere.

    But all of us ants can't see
    that all our DNA
    is deposited in you, the son,
    and from thereon the global, globular
    organism lives, breathes in tides,
    moves in traffic on Highway 281,
    preens its feathers in birdbaths,
    scrapes its velvet antlers on a tree,
    they are the dandelions, the fishes
    in the opaque ocean depths,

the lovers on their lover's paths,
fowl, reptile, plant, crustaceans,
all of your creations,
they are the organisms sprung from you,
us, them, and me.

175. Half of All, All of Half

Should I have a mere half my faculties,
should they be absent for one reason or another,
should I drive them like frontier mules past poor performance
into a feverish productivity, Father,

Would that not be equal to possessing all faculties,
safely bosomed, unthreatened, routinely accessed
and in this luxury not know it nor show it,
so, if using only half my measure fully,
would not all of half be equal to half of all?

176. Our Gifts

Lord,
We look at our gifts,
Christmas morning every day,
Easter in the woods today and tomorrow,
your biological resurrection among the weeds,
look out at our two acre organism,
communities of growth that are our gift wrapped packages
delivered by you, O Lord.

Like so many in the crowded field of exemplaries,
Saint Nicholas should have been here
on my pedestal porch,
looking at the gifts that fly and those that fall
and land into your bosom soil,
then come back again as recurrent gifts,
as you did.

177. The Features of Your Creatures

Lord,
Bless the eye that opens
flower like to embrace the honey light,
accepting the color of fall woods
with leaves spread across the spectrum,
bless the ear that hears
the wind in the trees,
the music of celestial spheres,
bless the tongue that among
the senses can taste a melon or a lemon,
bless the fingers that can feel,
even when the eyes have lost lens magic,
bless the nose that knows the rose
and its nasal echo,
bless them all, O Lord,
the features of your creatures

178. Our Chosen Sorrow

Father,
Only you know which way
we will go.
Will we continue to turn away
from you and so
head toward our chosen sorrow,
our disguised vanity,
or jump the treachery
and land on solid ground,
past this current,
ever recurring insanity?

179. Disappearing Into You

Lord,
I am feebly making my way toward you,
following you, watching for you,
listening to your mechanisms endlessly churning,
on my way toward you,
becoming you, finally, hopefully, lovingly burning,

disappearing into you, and with my breath
in, out, I say "Je-sus, Je-sus",
but now I am only me, and know
your power is greater than
the power that pulls me away from you
and towards a certainty of permanent death.

180. In You Alone

Father,
I rest in you alone,
my salvation, my rock
that brings peace and not discord,
not loneliness, coldness,
like a winter foot without a sock.

You are my strength,
my refuge from the storms
that not only sailors see.
Again and again you come
and rescue me.

I will do my best to be
your steward, your mouth
that speaks in tribute
to your majesty,
O Lord.
   From Psalms: 62

181. Summer Rain

Your trees wilt in heat,
in their own way weep,
leaves falling downward in disappointment.
Tree frogs surrender,
silent in murky shadows.
Dirt has turned to dust, cinnabar grasses to ocher,
summer shows no pity.
I dream of mountains,
spring streams and sweater weather.
Suddenly, the sky darkens to burnt blue,

a storm approaches with its bowling thunder,
a western wind whips, trees sway, the sun dips under cover,
then rain, sweet rain, your June jewel falling, wetting all.
What more than a tiger shark in still waters could make such a furrow
than this rain on sand and hills?
When it ceases tree frogs beg for more,
never satisfied,
crickets and their woodsy comrades contribute to a nightly chorus,
and I wonder if they all hear each other.

182. Our Greatest Mean

Father,
I applaud all the variations
of those who worship you.
They all have their own recipes.
You left us with no specific map,
wondering how to worship you,
you did this on purpose, Lord,
so that we would all compete and grow
and think that our team
has the correct approach and so,
I know you give your blessings
on all who claim allegiance to you.
I know they are all sincere,
so let us greet our greatest mean
that is you, O Lord.

183. The Vision of You

Lord,
Habakkuk cried out,
as we all do,
but he had not received the vision,
one of a way out of all this,
a way to peace that does not disappoint,
he had not yet the vision of you.

He had not the ways to stir
into flames, gifts from you, O Lord,
had not the vision that

amidst a flurry of fledgling woe
could know that you can blur
hard light falling into a tender eye,
that you can make the oceans still,
the winds vanish, ice melt, can make desert rain,
the heavens purr.
   From: Habakkuk 1:2

184. The Zacchaeus Tree

Father,
I'm in the sycamore tree
looking for you,
for your wind to brush my brow,
will you come up to me
or should I come down for you?

I would but I don't know how,
but I'm learning, on my knees,
that the view from one place
is no better than another,
it's the seeing that's
in the believing, in learning
the way you show yourself
amongst the leaves.
   From: Luke 19:1–10

7

July

185. The Sandy Shore

Storm warnings at sea,
Lord, I'm running,
not away but toward it,
into winds that can cut
an island like me in two,
but you told us to have no fear,
those of us who chose you.

Twisted, tangled, strangled
from above and below,
alien seed now in store,
varmint cells that eat the harvest corn,
sea cells of explosive wind,
Lord,
take me, throw me
toward the sandy shore.

186. Body Wars

O Lord,
Cancer comes and brings body wars,
a confederacy of cells secede
and break the body balance
of internal harmonies,
and then there is a need
for you to intercede
as you have done for me
more than once.

> Father, I know
> that again and again you have rescued me,
> steered me away from calamity,
> loss, friction from lateral gravity,
> prevented the stains of dour hours
> that could have accompanied my moments
> when I saw the white buffalo.

187. What They Have to Say

> There are those with mighty brushes
> and they are attempting, striving, never sleeping,
> to paint the world gray,
> leading us into a moral desert, weeping.
> They say that you are no different, Lord,
> than any others who claim holiness, to be God's son,
> they say that all faiths are the same,
> so, to them be done,
> but we will not, should not listen,
> to what they have to say.
>
> They have been wrong before
> as they are now,
> with their universal equivalences
> and are smug when they kowtow
> to proven precarious remedies of the tongue,
> because the souls and manes
> of still free horses, the old, young,
> still manage to outrun them
> and manage to resist the notion of rubber truth,
> in you, or anything else, O Lord.

188. Beauty is Peace

> Lord,
> We walk away from times,
> from what brought us through
> our forefather's passages,
> their nails for hats we used for hanging,
> common binders their soups' own roux,

settlers', wanderers' cup of independence
washing in the ages' stew,
we turn away with less than that
for reasons poor, foolish, complex,
we change but not for good, we vex
and stray from a provider ages old,
our strengths wane, we strengthen doubt,
should we now be here without
the Attica dream that built domes and marble men?
We toss away the lasting wreath,
we stand and refuse to sit,
in chairs turned by lathes again,
for beauty is truth,
and no peace here absent it.

189. When We Go Alone

Lord,
You have given to us
our own decisions,
with or without you,
and when we go with you
as our forefathers insisted,
we are heirs to providence
but when we go alone
and let your spirit die
with your loving grace resisted,
we suffer as a people
and wonder why.

190. Dogs

They are about as close to us
as close can get,
can be taught to fetch,
shake, lye down and sit.

They've been lying down by our side
since loin cloth, bear skin times,
when we hunted and gathered
and the one who would come to show us

how to manage, survive, prosper, abide,
had yet to be born,
and they were there too over the lands
of the early, puppy earth.

They were there for the Caddo, thus,
tracker allies to those hunting game,
protectors, warning them of enemy approaches,
there for the peasant, the gentry,
obedient by the sides of their kings, us.

And when you came, Lord,
they were there too in lands and with peoples
who were remote, isolated
from the drum of amelioration
towards what was possible
and had never heard of you.

They are here, now, by our feet,
adoring us as nothing else does,
our gift from the Almighty
who turned a wolf into a sheep.

191. Voyage of Life

Lord,
Thomas Cole had it right,
that we all travel through
and down a river of four seasons,
that our childhood is our due,
when tendrils grow, advance, legs crawl,
get longer, walk, then dance.
Our blossoms coincide
with gradual growing reasons.

In summer we become youth,
grasses prosper and we run

through them, growth spurts reflect
the wheat, corn of our bodies
that expand as surely as do wings
of early doves and late faun.

The fall visits with cooler times,
we and all your creatures now grown,
migratory birds have matured, risen and flown,
a zenith here and everywhere,
reaching its peak and passing on
to prepare for frost.

In the winter of our times
we mimic trees and miss some things
we had in summers, now lost,
like Yellowstone elks we endure abrasions
of rock hard cold and memories of springs
and like under humus seeds
wait for our resurrections.

192. Thank You for the Rock

Lord, thank you for the rock
where we sat and watched
the mountain water roll over bottom stones
polished slick and egglike
by rapid currents and slow time.

Thank you for the trout we never caught
but watched as they zig zagged through eddies
and darted under cold shadows,
usually just out of casting reach,
swimming in the same water over and over.

Thank you for the rock
covered in green scaly moss
and to the tiny violet
defying all probability
and prospering in a crack.

Thank you for the op at the top
of the goodtime bank
of recollections, for being then
and there in sprucy woods
where nothing ever changed.

Thank you for the rock
that presided over those misty woods
of hemlock canopies and milky fog
with a virgin river rolling between boulders,
that looked to have been dropped by giants.

193. Where Are You?

Father, so many ask
where you are.
Where are you now that we need you most,
as if we haven't always?
Where were you in the trenches of WWI?
Where were you in the Great Depression?
Where were you in WWII and other wars
when men, not you, slaughtered other men?

So many ask, where are you
when our loved ones suffer,
when children are abused or abandoned?
I know that you allow man
his free reign, which often results in calamities
not of you but of another,
whose pedigree is hate, greed, lust, vengeance.

These are not qualities of you.
Should you completely govern our lives,
where then be our wills?
Should you dictate our every move,
where then our growth?

You are there but so is he
who plans evil in the hearts of all.

Thank you for our freedoms.
Help us to not blame you when we fall.

194. THE RAINS CAME

The rains came and emptied the skies.
The water rose above banks,
above roads, docks, bridges,
above the edges of normal levels,
it eroded the bank's soft ridges,
challenged the dam,
confused the fishes with muddy space.
It rose above the hills, drowned the sun and shadows below.
Lord, you gave the drought
a fatal blow.
Thank you, Lord, for the rains.

195. TRUE JUSTICE FOR JOE

Lord,
We don't have much
and what we have is short
in the sea of time,
we struggle, wait in line
for our eventual strife,
we are bruised and need you,
all of us with unkind cuts endured.

There is no reason we can see,
for the good, the young
to leave early, while
scoundrels die of old age,
but they, not the undeserving,
will have to pay their onerous wage,
for our justice is man-made,
so with its unfair faults,
but yours is true and right,
so, knowing, we make it through an empty night,
without those we love and lose,
we wait for a new life to begin,

their memories live on and do not fade,
until we see them yet again.
>
> For Joe Knafla. July, 2009

196. Accept Him Lord

Accept him, Lord,
into your kingdom,
even though he took his earthly life,
give him another.
He was young and blind to consequences,
and left us all without a goodbye,
in the night when we were all sleeping,
took away his hope and ours for him
and left us all weeping,
wishing we could have reached him,
comforted him in his sorrow.
Accept him Lord,
into your keeping.

197. Lead Me like a Horse

O Lord,
Lead me like a horse
by bit and bridle
to what I am supposed to do,
that I may not waste
my remaining days
in selfish pursuits,
ignoring your grace,
not working on my weaknesses,
but instead getting stronger
in you.

198. What You Make Does Not Change

Lord Jesus,
There is one who furrows
underground like a mole,
eats the roots of truth,
wilts the burning bush

and like a spirit worm,
infects, contaminates the soul.

You know his name
and so do I.
He hides and seeks,
sacks the city of faith,
takes down temples of your word,
brick by brick,
and camouflages his lie.

He says there is no truth,
that we should just stop seeking,
he's said it ever so,
he loosens adherences, says
they can be changed even though
what's true is true because
what you make does not change,
what he makes and we make does.

199. WE FOLLOW YOU

Lord,
We follow you through
vacant or full fields,
may differ in our sky views,
some in sage, some in sprucy places,
swampy or snowy spaces, mountain plateaus,
even in early evening woods or daybreak dews.

We follow and see you
in all that moves, grows or not,
in rock, spider, loblolly pine,
leopard, lemon, ice crystal,
in tides that churn each wave anew,
in expansions, shrinkings, stations stable, or rot.

We follow you in various robes, hats,
in sun, sleet, wind, rain,
expected to love each other and that's
why we should shun those

who disparage followers of you,
who break your love
that is a never ending chain.

200. Surgery

I stepped into the river of incompleteness,
remembering an intactness
that was no more,
into a current capable of carrying me
downstream to my eventual end,
I was punctured, bashed against rocks, sore,
I called out to you, O Lord,
to take me across to the distant bank,
I endured in fitful sleep and found
I could almost swim again,
and reached an eddy where the current waned,
I called again and spoke your name
when I reached the promised ground.

201. Blessing in Flight

Lord,
I saw you in the hummingbird wing
when he flew through the spray
from my garden hose,
I heard you sing,
so I am now in the company of those
to whom you have chosen to reveal yourself.
I sensed your effervescence in his buzz
as he levitated before the hose's spray,
I'm on my knees now, Lord, to pray
that your presence is a blessing in flight.

202. After Always Being Something

Lord,
Where has his spirit gone,
the one I felt beside me as a boy?
Did it vanish with his body
into his grassy grave,

dissolved like his flesh into
nothing but a milky memory?
Where is that presence
that helped form me?
Is it gone forever,
like a loved one drowned
and unfound at sea?

I believe it is with you, Lord,
because even though he spent
years denying you,
in his last days he changed
from his fears of becoming nothing,
after always being something,
he became a believer
and is now heaven sent.

203. THE STURDY ROCK OF YOU

The foibles of false choices
keep rocking, going, muffling chances loud, free,
of hearing royal voices
of tongues that speak what is true
rather than what they wish to be.

I pledge to avoid fractious rantings
from those who do not hear
sweet peace performed by the organist
inside the inner ear,
to avoid the tarnished liquid
disguised as truth but onion skin thin,
that differs in its longevity
to the prolonged purity of the sturdy rock
of you, the maker, and your glorious flock.

204. A DEVIOUS WEED

Lord,
There has never been, and to our woe,
in the hearts of men and women

a permanent peace that we can know,
instead a tempting to take,
break tranquility like a twig,
someone wanting what someone else has,
someone pushing their will, not yours
on his or her neighbor,
someone small wanting to be big,
raising armies, massing demands,
someone doing something that they
would condemn others for doing,
all the time pursuing,
crafting, cultivating a devious weed,
a seed that grows to power, greed,
thinking they are exempt from history,
losing the scent, the trail
to your love, O Lord.

205. A Chance

Lord,
I was there and walked
down streets millennia worn,
where the sand paper of time had stolen
the edges of stones,
down Paul-walked streets,
Peter-climbed hills,
the arenas still there
where torture was entertainment
until you came around,
Lord,
and gave us a chance,
still unclaimed by some.

206. Should We Go There

Lord,
Should we venture
wherever we would want to go,
we should wander over ground
where you would wish us not.

Without boundaries we get lost, lose direction,
are victims of an infection
that cannot tell up from down.

Should there ever be an offer suggesting
idleness to be the norm,
our youth always eager to conform
would take the bait
of any pleasure path away from you.

Should we go there,
there's more loss than gain,
a short ecstatic burst
for temporal carnal rides,
treat others as the worst,
are not quite ready for full freedom,
end up not knowing you, ourselves,
or anyone else.

207. Cellular Pirate

Lord,
Here he comes with an aberration in his groin,
needing your help to go on
and he is one of yours
who has lived his life the way you suggest.
Please, Lord, protect him and all others
who are yours and rescue those
who aren't and make them so,
or is that our job?

He has that hideous growth that
so many of us succumb to,
growing inside him like a cellular pirate,
expanding, destroying, feeding on what you have made
with such extraordinary detail.
Its growth is the handiwork of the dark one,
consuming sections of your divine design.
Please, Lord, put a stop to it
and let him continue.

208. Before We Are Taken Home

Turning and turning in the spiraling mire,
our lives consumed with churning races,
we fill our sails and encounter shoals
but set our sights on something higher.

We descend trying trails, ignore warning signs,
walk past urgings to do what's right.
We seldom remember history's ugly lessons,
and end up re-inventing our own times.

We sail to soothe a death alone,
ours in the dirt of final places
and for our sins only we can atone,
we pray for others to join us, Lord,
before we are taken home.

209. Double the Sight

Father,
In the shadow of your wings
I shout for joy
at the light of solar response,
your son the sun blood of leaves.
I saw your face in a dream.
You had three eyes in a mirror,
one looking up, one looking down, and one at me,
it was cold and condensation on the glass
looked like tears from your eyes,
and your reflection doubled the sight
that I could see.

210. Because

Because of the unending,
sometimes unbearable sadness of being,
because we lose so much in seeing
along with our gains we try to save,
because of obstacles in our path
that you are always giving

to keep us from inertia and decay,
would we not possess any urge
to grow, expand in our living,
would we have never emerged
from our stone cold caves,
would we have ever made you proud of us
the way we are when our children excel?
Thank you, O Lord,
for making us what we have become.

211. Tumbling Along Contented

They're tumbling along more contented
than us, those living creatures
that do not have the blessings
of conscience bestowed upon humans
by you, O Lord,

They sprout their budding leaves,
burst open from chrysalis tombs into flight,
search with owl eyes for sustenance
in a hungry, moonless night,
spawn in weedy shallows,
defy gravity with figure-eight hummingbird wings,
suckle their spotted fawn offsprings,
all knowing what to do on cue,
tumbling along, contented
with what they are
and what they're here to do.

212. Your Approval is His Measure

Father,
Many are the troubles of the just man.
He seeks to do right when wrong
would bring him treasure.
He turns away from temptation
and does his best.
Your approval is his measure.

He does not seek unworthy gifts,
turns away from greed,
from false witness, impure pleasure.
He turns away from what he knows is wrong
by the altimeter in his heart that you gave him
and tries his best.
Your approval is his measure.
        From Psalms 34:19

213. About Forever

Father, what do those who
do not believe in you
have to say about forever
and the consequences of death,
about the moment just past
their last breath?

What do those who
seldom give a thought
to why they are here
have to say about forever
which is in this room now, and near?

What do those think who
believe that their own deeds
are enough to justify the space they fill,
are they waiting for a sign,
for you to show them the way
while they wait until
their last lingering moment?

214. You Gave Us You

Lord, in July your little shad fish
shimmy on the surface of the cool lake water,
sometimes they swim, minnows in a sea of peril
and make it to become larger fishes,
sometimes they are victims
of shark-bass and the waters erupt,

a feeding frenzy seen too at sea
but you, Lord, gave the shad
a weapon for the defense of its progeny,
you allow them to spawn at dawn like aqua mosquitoes
shimmying in glass clear, smooth
water, mirror calm blue
and you allow them to outpopulate
the percentages of their casualties.
You gave us a weapon, too, Lord,
you gave us you.

215. A Stone into Bread

When we are strapped with worry,
our plight in perilous straits,
ones we love in pain or sorrow,
we lift our hearts to you, O Lord
and focus on a hope for tomorrow.

We should not resort to doubt,
to question, allow the dark one
to convince us of suspicion,
or question what your motive is about.
We will not put you to a test, O Lord,
but instead, remember what you said
and that you, even you
did not choose to turn
a stone into bread.
   From: Matthew 4:3

216. I'll Fly Away

I'll fly away
O Lord,
the way migrant birds do,
disappearing and not appearing
until a new season, like you.

I'll fly away in the morning
or not, and nest with others
who have flown,

my end my own
towards you,
with a direction seated, repeated
every day by those who choose,
with a direction like a goose in formation,
with a direction hardwired towards you.

8

August

217. A Puff of Air

    Emerging first from submersion,
    blessed wet and humbled, given a boat
    for sailing latter water
    but found the boat without sail,
    decades spent casually conducting,
    constructing a wind glove,
    seam here, there in paint, canvas,
    stitching to-be propellant from random threads,
    heaven wagon transport, rocket wishes,
    wind widowed upon silent water,
    dead in a feckless sea, marooned in spent spans
    while sleeping, wondering, should I perish in the parish?

    Then swept in silence,
    not need watching peacefully in place,
    when behind an ear a puff of air just passed
    wondering had I seated sitting centered
    under a ceiling fan or vent but no,
    air came from nowhere past my ear
    a sound I heard , or maybe didn't hear,
    "Was that a coyote yipping last night or not?
    Was that honey lip or imagined sweetness?
    Did I see a light, comet fuse, racing star,
    or was that a floater in my eye?"
    Was this the wind that whipped water into blue meringue,
    the puff that disperses daffodil dust,

that blows the candle fire from children's cakes
when their gusto cannot douse the flame?
Puffs felt not imagined just passed will linger, last.
Sailing is as supportable as not,
I sail or sit alone, shore bound.

218. Your Truth, Spirit, Fire

You will know us if
we love one another
but we are tarnished, Lord,
with our judgment that
is not yours, but
should love our sister, brother,
lest we become victims
of your enemies.

How are we to defend ourselves
from those who spurn love
for their own advances?
Should we submit to tyranny,
to the loveless, and take our chances?

Elegance and beauty but not love
can be crushed by a boot,
what crushings should we allow
and when should we stand up
against a malignant root?

Love is a strong tonic
for even the loveless,
yet there is nothing naysayers more desire
than for us to not defend
your truth, spirit, fire.

219. Who Knows Where?

Lord,
We know we go to who knows where,
we pray for tracks on honey lanes,
we keep our hope in projections high,
hoping it sustains and never wanes
of seeing you in the bye-and-bye, there
along with all the others we once loved
who have gone to we know where,
to be with you, our fathers, mothers,
we go but who knows when
to meet the crowds of those
who have chosen you
and who you chose.

220. A New Moses

Lord Jesus,
You gave us an option
to enslave ourselves if we choose
or choose not, though the sword
is a mighty persuader
and sometimes our choices are made for us.

We can will and make into law
a defiance of that will,
delegate it to others
in the manner it has been taken from us in the past
by leaders who promise us that
they won't deceive.

Why do we never see
the will-grabbers in any age?
Why do we let them tame us, shame us,
coerce us into a will not ours?
Only you offer forgiveness when we misstep,
others offer punishment.
Will you punish us too, as before?
Lord, send us now a new Moses.

221. This Blue Sky There All Along

Have rediscovered the silky sheen, Lord,
of this big blustery sky, there all along,
while I peered at earth and prayed,
with its four acts and endless faces,
spring stirrings, nubile growth,
full fall palette the woods around,
punishing summers in Naples yellow fields,
rock hard winter ground.

The big blue sky hovers over the pier
where shellcracker bream cower in shade,
turtles occasionally come up for air,
stick their horny noses above the water
to observe the airy world above,
which was there all along
while I was looking at the water times two,
the lake epoxy-still and being
a calm echo far and across to the other side
where the sun drowns each evening,
apple-dunked into the trees
to the accompaniment of birds
on their way home.

222. Giving All

There are those
who have given
their only all,
made a sacrifice
when everyone else
either gave one,
or a few but not all,
all the time
and I wonder,
just how much
I have given,
and is it enough for you,
O Lord.

223. THE SWELLINGS

Church bells, fog,
birth swells, dawn.
You come to me in light or thunder,
in the shadow valley, lipped and loaded voice,
requesting reverence for the suffering
in blood running rivers,
from idea to form to idea,
you manifest when swellings commence.

Pernicious pseudo patrons are here
who place you less than least,
who fall again and again,
without comfort of breath and beauty,
bridge burners all
whose sum is not
swellings but death.

In pink moon seasons
swellings surge and subside,
the woods are dressing
for their up and coming show,
history grows, the moon
is casting its spell over the tide.

You sacrificed for sacred essence
in turbulence on a nail.
Your name has been murdered,
glorified, deified, scorned
and felt, with your answers in oceans
yet you prevail,
thus none naught but which you made,
sometimes misgiven, sometimes not,
but should you twice to offer
to our sister and brother
you would say, "Rediscover."

224. Help Me or Retrieve Me

Abba one
Abba all
Abba Father come,
holy spirit,
should you call
me home I will see
your divine face and all those I loved
who have gone away from me,
so come, Father,
and help me or retrieve me.
Amen.

225. Soldiers Today

Big talk and spirit driven,
I say in the manner of all
your billion minions
who ever offered their throats
rather than deny you in the Coliseum,
we know your soldiers today, we see them,
they are the ones who believe in miracles,
that they were not just long ago legends
and are not bought but given
nor trapped by ages,
they know they've paid their wages,
and know too that you, Lord,
as those who saw you the second time knew,
are the only one to ever come back
from the terminal stages.

226. For All Ages

Lord Jesus,
You make known your might to us
for those listening.
We are in discourse of your glory,
much time has passed, years like turned pages,
we know your story
and that yours is a kingdom for all the ages.

You have set the world ablaze,
have made divisions everlasting
between those who follow you
and those who follow nothing,
between those who believe
there is a message in the waking world
that should be heard,
and those who do not, who fear it
or refuse to hear it.

Over a long train of centuries
we have come still warring, coveting, lusting,
some still marching to their own music,
still believing only in themselves,
ignoring the news that
the soldiers of the swords
who always come with
a power for peace-busting,
have not yet come for them.
Lord, I pray that they
will hear your call and come forward.

We have had our chances
to hear your news from early fathers, desert monks,
martyrs, emperors, kings, queens,
peasants, in simple rooms and palaces,
small gatherings and grand cathedrals
we sit, stand, kneel in pews,
and have for two millennia.
So now is the time if there ever was,
to accept the obvious truth
of your good news.
           From Psalms 145:12

227. A Less than Reckless Ramble Fizzling

Lord Jesus,
How will the road ahead fare?
Will I descend pinnacle hill
where spring greens are topping
and glide downward and with
leaves flying in autumn air,
a pleasant ride south, slow and low
to a valley and a gentle stopping?

Will there be a rocky incline instead,
with angels flown and tigers at my back?
Will I be bereft of sweetness
or the mouths of children kissing missing,
imprisoned by faulty movement, marooned on a bed?

Whatever way the terminal terrains play,
whether peaceful or tumultuous ride,
down the hill of this now being,
down the stretch a swagger less than sizzling,
down the path a still solicitous seeing,
down the valley a less than reckless ramble fizzling,
with you, there, on my side.

228. Help Our Children

Lord,
Please help our children go forth,
prosper and multiply
with children of their own
to propel us into a future with you, in you.

Our numbers are shrinking, Lord,
our children are fewer,
our world filling with those
who not only deny you
but are hostile to you and your people.

Help us increase our numbers, Lord,
rid us of the scourge of ending lives
before they even begin,
lost lives who could have been
followers of you, Lord.

229. You Are Here

Lord,
Thanks for the feast
of living in the holy air
of your presence in all things,
at the jay's last twilight call,
thunder that gives us drama skies,
for rain that anoints the roots,
for your mix-master rotation of days,
yeast that rises soul and bread and seed,
blood music with the heart on drums,
for each breath gift from you,
for not only believing but knowing
that you are here.

230. Backyard Birds

Lord,
Your mourning doves are in the branches with a cant
with singing in the trees and a coo,
much like the barn owl with his nocturnal chant,
"who cooks for you, who cooks for you?"
Your grackles cackle with much ado,
back and forth, from here to there
and together I hear a bird chorus
with each announcing his all,
his space and limb.

I know that this is you speaking too,
calling all with a disguised presence,
the males fluff and strut and woo,
you populate the branches and skies,
fill the heavens with migratories

on their way to a better place
on a secluded sun bleached beach
where they will squawk, strut and dance,
I'm waiting for my encounter too,
for my migration.
I'm waiting for my chance.

231. You Are There

Lord,
In deep dark water
where catfishes sleep,
you are there,
in alpine air where
rocky tops and clouds meet,
you are there,
in wide plateaus where antelope romp for miles,
in places where the ages
have cut the canyons deep,
in droughts when water shrinks,
in floods where it rages,
you are there.

In thunder, rain, sun,
You are there until
Our short jog has jogged and gone,
In days, nights, winds fierce, still,
Waiting for us to come to you
Carried down the terminal aisles.

232. They Are Many

Lord,
One was so consumed
with the pursuit of power,
that narcotic that usually separates
the seeker from the flock
no matter if their actions
or designed or on a whim

or what they call themselves,
they are many, common,
and we always fall for them.

Another was so consumed
with the pursuit of wealth,
that narcotic that usually separates
the seeker from the flock,
he calls himself comfortable,
he can be many and may not know
what being rich is.

Another was so consumed
with carnal pleasure or drink,
those narcotics that usually separate
the seeker from the flock
and he or she was, is always hungry
for something that cannot bring peace,
they are many and may not know
what being contented is.

None of these may have lived
by knowing that,
should others do what they do,
what they are about to do
at any given time,
would not be best for all,
not even just a few.

233. THE STREAM OF THE SKY

Sunshine, maybe rain time,
will we be in the hay meadow more?
Buildings, glass and steel made,
will we work on the fortieth floor?
Your door is my ceiling,
Lord, will you look down on me?
Seeing, looking upward,
waiting for the clouds to go by.

Hurry, hurry, never worry,
ready now if ever to see,
waiting, ever gaiting,
coasting in the stream of the sky.

234. An Even Greater Loss

Lord,
We wonder why the good go
and the wicked triumph.
We are confused and do not know,
yet trust that your wisdom
even amidst our losses
is for the best, lest
we revert to animal urges
and devour each other,
which would be an ever greater loss.

235. The Sun Is Dying

The sun is dying in the trees,
over the water the light diminishing
just as it has done forever,
as it did over Palatine Hill,
when emperors sat on thrones
watching the day's passing,
over the ocean's deep, expansive blue
with sailors gliding over seas,
the darkness amassing,
just as it did on Calvary on that dreadful day,
just as it did over Bethlehem
the day you were born, Lord,
and the heavens delivered three stars,
just as it did at Antietam,
the yellow light illuminating the corpses,
its rays filtered through smoke,
just as it did on the Mount of Olives
the day you spoke
and told us the way we should be.

236. Bag of Rocks

Father,
It gets easier incrementally
as though I am carrying around
a bag of rocks
and lose one each day.

She left without warning,
leaving me here without her.
On the first day I awoke wet eyed,
a new withoutness here within
with the sun rising in the window,
more rocks were picked up then.

I am praying for a day
when I no longer feel the weight
and thoughts of her are sporadic,
when I can return to a time
when mother mourning was absent
and I only remember the rocks.

237. To Ask, What?

Lord,
How could some be
so devoid of you,
their steel hearts
cold as winter glass,
their predatory hungers
fed with others' blood,
their anger over their anger
at what they are
and what they are not?

Lord,
Do you leave them
to their own devises,
their cruel capacities,
greed that only takes,

never makes, never revises?
Do you speak to them
yet they hear you not?
Do you rattle the rushes
for them too, attempt to pursue
yet their malice can only grow,
their hearing never noticing,
never turning from their fury
to ask, what?

238. The Passion

Lord, there is a passion
for tides that often lead us away from you,
for the truth is sometimes victim
to fashion,
that like a flood takes all or most
along with its false hopes
that started out as mere rain.

There is a passion to belong,
the young fear exclusion from peers,
will trade truth for a penny,
their herd takes them with it,
sometimes are gone for years,
only to never return
to your truth, or any.

There is a passion that blinds,
that says the pack says so,
and so, so do I,
even when it brings harm, delusion,
for those who go with the flow.

239. What You Do

Father of all,
We must avoid thinking
that nothing is annual,
as opposed to perennial

but our doings are temporary,
and yours are not.

What you do you have done
from the beginning when
you gave us the word,
then again when it was made flesh,
embodied under the linens of you, O Lord.

What you do is the original force
that put all in motion,
orbiting, evolving, bettering itself, ourselves,
often through progressions that we can't see,
so everything is on its way somewhere,
ant, antelope, alligator, you, me.

240. STILL, EAGLES

Our progeny is our shadow
projecting when we are no longer here,
we want them to be worthy
of transference of form,
of running with the time ball,
downfield, handing it off,
so that it progresses
and does not have to punt.

We want our progeny
to not strike out in the bottom of the 9th
with the bases loaded, oh no,
but to reach home
even when dust is suspended in air,
where you are, Lord, a place where
your peace placates the pernicious,
the sometimes here-to-for's
and everyone gets to bat and have
a chance to be a hero.

Should our progeny, or ourselves
strike out, you will help us, Lord,
not to be lemmings but eagles,
missing a fish here and there
but still, eagles.

And should we lose our progeny, O Lord,
we're at a loss for what to do,
but we have our pictures of days warm, fair,
know of the living roulette wheel
and know too that our progeny
are eagles, still
and we'll see them when we see you.

241. The Blessed Arts

Thank you Lord,
for giving us the mighty men
and women who have given us
pleasures for our eyes,
the magnificent Michelangelo
making stone speak,
for Titian and his dark depiction of you
suffering on the cross,
for Rembrandt and his spirit paint,
that showed the souls of his sitters,
for Okeefe and her cosmos of flowers.

Thank you Lord,
for the musicians who have strummed
the cords of our hearts,
for the poets who have carved
life into word,
thank you Lord for the blessed arts.

242. Sing a New Song

Turning and tumbling in the toiling tide
that swallows sea litter
and moves all along,
a current that wraps the victim

like a spider would in water,
you, Lord,
are the oxygen in the wave
here to endower, retrieve, save,
and we choose to move along with you
in this swift and always ending race
and "sing a new song unto the Lord,"
or we can choose
to wash up on the shore
without grace.
        From Psalms 114:9

243. Road Rabbit

Lord,
Help us with what we intend to do.
Let us do it without losing what we have made
with your grace only.
We have done what we have done only because you allowed it.
We could have been a rabbit in the road with wheels approaching,
instead, we survived and tried to deliver something worthwhile,
not just for our own gratification
but contributions for others.
Allow us to continue.
We all have gifts, even the rabbit.
Guide us in how to use them.
Amen.

244. Solid Sand

O Lord,
In those moments when the day
has a little night in it
and the night a little of day,
and it's hard to tell if the light
has been impregnated with darkness
or the darkness bleached with light,
I dream I float just barely offshore,
drifting with undulating tides
that are like wet minutes to my days.

Lord,
Keep me from drifting off into the sea,
marooned in misdirection away from you,
never to ever return.
Keep my feet on solid sand
and safely on land,
where I can do whatever it is
I am supposed to do.

245. Almighty Inevitable

Lord,
Even an iron-hard hematite stone,
given enough time,
washes downstream into red dust in solution,
driven by curly currents and the Almighty Inevitable.
Anything once started
eventually stops, whether
in moments or millennial spans.

Tomorrow, the start stops,
a new start starts,
the red rock cools
and waits for the stream,
motion begets stillness,
waking makes a current
and the breaking night a dream.

Tomorrow is a new times time,
the first leg of a many legged course,
singletrees are hitched, oxen are snorting,
chances of peril and peace await,
an old beginning ending,
the Almighty Inevitable beckons,
"Pilgrims, prepare your wagons."

So we are neophytes again,
old birds out of the egg
heading west, gambling with time,

vulnerable to circumstance and pointed things,
fragile, with wet wings,
dreaming of flying and
praying to you, O Lord, for our passage.

246. Your Grace Only

The mouth of the just murmurs wisdom,
even though he may not be learned,
he senses the wicked way
and turns from it,
feels the righteous path and sees
where it leads,
waits in silence and prays
for his wayward brothers and sisters
on his knees.

Even the birds have learned
to not eat some insects, fearing poison,
but some men sometimes surrender
to their damaging wishes, unconcerned.
O Lord, let us all acknowledge
that it is your grace that saves
and your grace only that frees
all of us from pathetic graves.
From: Psalms 37:30

247. Three Are Greater Than One

You are with us,
Lord, when we suffer
we can remember you
and when we don't,
praise you that we don't suffer.
You are our map
while those without
become travelers lost in woods,
at the very least in their moments of death.
Have we no hope
the grave is a lonelier hole

since we will never know,
we hope in you the son,
your father and spirit,
and have hope here and there,
for three are greater than one.

9

September

248. Not A Spigot

Lord Jesus,
You asked the blind man Bartimaeus
to get up and walk to you
as a measure of his effort.
You ask us all to extend a request,
to make an effort too,
and that we not just ask
blessings for only ourselves
or only when we are in dire places,
but also for our sisters and brothers.
We're asking for your graces,
but you are not a spigot
to be turned on only when
we are with thirst.
You are a fountain that
we must walk to with our needs,
and the needs of others.
        From Mark 10:46–52

249. Well Designed Kingdom

Lord,
The tanager flaunts his red
and chirps in bird-speak.
He lets us know his presence
at the bird bath
where he splashes in joy

while only a few feet away
hummingbirds do battle at the feeder
like airplanes at Midway,
spending more time flying,
defying gravity, protecting space,
than they do eating.
All this goes on every day, Lord,
in your well designed kingdom.

250. The Trail of Time

The trail of time trickles on,
a debris carrying current
swirling through the centuries,
carrying Egyptian monuments, mummies,
Greek statues in contrapposto,
Roman centurions, chariots, emperors,
kings, monarchs, martyrs, Gothic cathedrals,
carrying armies marching at Tours,
Gettysburg, Waterloo, Normandy,
carrying sorrow, joy, great achievement,
Sistine Chapels, guillotines,
scientists in laboratories,
carrying the litter of endeavors,
the flotsam of the ages,
all eventually to be,
carrying us down the roiling river
into the sea,
unto you,
O Lord.

251. Rain and Other Favors

Father, it was Texas hot,
the trees were weeping, azaleas wilting,
the ground was cracking,
the sun baking the garden green,
when you made your presence
with a long, cooling rain
and the plant and animal kingdom sang.

O Lord,
Is this your way of making us appreciate
what we have by taking it from us?
If so, I will consider any loss
as a message from you
that I should not take for granted
even the smallest of your favors.

252. The Stretch

Lord,
The stretch begins with birth announcements,
infants with vinyl smooth skin,
unfocused eyes and some endowed sin,
yet no willed corruption of your trust,
instead, a celebration of your greatest gift.

The stretch, tiny in time's capacity,
ends with obituary and mourners
remembering it and its worth,
and sometimes you mollify one with the other,
trading a child for a mother,
sister or brother,
a jewel given and a treasure taken.

Lord, let my last stretch be the longest,
at least my loved ones' not forsaken,
instead, traded with another of your gifts.

253. The Way the World Begins

This is the way the world begins,
not with a bang but with a whack
upside the head or downside the bottom,
a cold codfish wallop
or hand that spanks the newborn
into winces at florescent space.

This is the way the world begins
with lively cellular jolts
that ignite life from fluids,

the essence of is,
our being's nuts and bolts.

From this magic moment onwards,
the burst of bloom
goes forth from our mother's womb,
we go through our cycles
like nature's trees in winter, spring, summer, fall,
and this is how we all
end, from nothing into something into nothing,
unless we have you, O Lord.

254. The Truth that is You

Lord, we've tried it without you
and it did not work.
We tried pursuing our own passions,
taking us to wherever they would
and they took us to some unpleasant places.

We tried making our own rules
independent of you, ran our own races,
spontaneously building roads, bridges
that went no where except to tyranny, lost promise,
to our own Waterloo.

Lord, help us to learn
from the mistakes of others,
from infections of our own hubris,
from always present false messiahs,
from a recycled falsehood that always smothers
the truth that is you, O Lord.

255. Let Me Be

Father, fling me from Tarpeian rocks,
pluck out an eye, steal a limb or two,
savage me while I wait
for a new Edict of Milan,

I'm choosing what I think over what I feel,
trying to distinguish
the fake from the real.

Lord, do what you will with me,
but I beg you let me be
at least for a time that is not now,
so that I can remain here to love
you and those you have given to me.

256. Thank You for Our Soul

Father in heaven,
your hummingbird knows how
to defy gravity with his wings,
the secretive summer tanager knows
how to hide when he sings,
the caterpillars know how to imitate leaves,
the duck floats on freezing water
with his insulated feathers warm as a glove,
plants sense solar geometries,
your camel sits on the sand on his knees,
your pair of mockingbirds around their nest
know how to mimic love.

Father, all is ordered, sustained in time,
your packaged design revolving
with each player knowing his or her part,
their habits passed down even
with those without blood.
You gave some wings, some gills,
some speed and some strength,
you allowed some to accommodate stifling heat,
some live through the arctic cold,
O Lord, thank you for giving us what we have,
thank you for our soul.

257. Throne with Wheels

Horses in summer fields swat flies,
clouds move east to west,
the lily has its run and dies
but she doesn't care,
her usefulness is spent,
she waits for permanent rest.

She's outlived all her friends, relatives too,
her only solace an absence of memory
of how it used to be,
to compare to her current
nursing home throne with wheels.

Approaching her century span now
she's a queen of ages,
sees little, hears less,
spends her out of focus, soundless time
mostly in bed under cover,
can't remember me, or them, or then,
or even her sixty year lover.

She sits in her penal wheel chair,
her sentence for only living too long,
can't read, hear music or voices,
she's down to breathing
and not-breathing choices.

The nurses bring her drugs and food,
but she can't taste
even what she used to love.
The sun comes through her window and reveals
her white hair, sunken skin,
she waits, vacantly for nothing,
in her nursing home throne with wheels.

She used to be your dutiful servant, Lord,
lived according to your plan,
had few vices, many friends,
but she has no doubt forgotten you,
who she is, her house, her life, her man,
but you have not forgotten her, Lord.

258. Instead, Grace and Mercy

You do not bring us justice
Lord, instead, grace and mercy,
for if you did so we would have no reason
to seek it, if all was predictable
there'd be no reason for faith,
instead you give us grace,
grateful for this moment and the next,
you give us peace
and because all is not pre-known
without toil, without tests
of our allegiance to you,
instead, we suffer and you give us mercy,
but tonight, Lord,
this one time, again,
give us justice.

259. Making Space Visible

At first light, silent stillness,
one by one birds awake,
initiated by a lone cardinal,
owls on their way home,
day bleeds yellow
as the source approaches horizon weeds,
and then all comes into view
as it does here, now
over the once brightening,
now crumbling Acropolis,
or over waters watched
by New World sailors,
it illuminates slowly, eternally.

Soon, deer slide through the woods
as though they have been bathed in oil,
they appear like ghosts
with stealth color and movement,
white tail in running mode
a crucial joy it is to see
your lighting candle, O Lord,
making space visible.

260. Leaning Forward

Ours is not to understand
but to stand, leaning forward in our chores
into whatever is left of our lives.
The only other onerous choice
is to abandon what life itself adores
which is, life itself,
the stuff of growth's nomenclature.

How could we possibly comprehend
truckloads of bodies retrieved
from evil tyrannies of some men, some nature,
despots, disasters, tragedies then and now?
We weep for all but mostly for those
who had no say in their circumstance.
We continue on, leaning forward somehow,
with faith in you, O Lord.

261. Our Kingdom Too?

Lord,
The Babylonians imprisoned the Jews
and you took away their kingdom;
the Romans crucified you and your brothers,
burned the temple in Jerusalem
and you took away their kingdom;
the Byzantines slaughtered thirty thousand in the hippodrome,
and you took away their kingdom;
the Aztecs sacrificed thousands,
their hearts beating in brown hands

and you took away their kingdom and lands;
the Nazis killed six million or more
and you took away their thousand year Reich
and left it at history's closed door;
and in our own time,
we have denied millions of pre-born lives,
more than all the others combined;
will you take away our kingdom too?

262. Into Eternity

Lord,
I have asked and I have found
solace in you.
I have knocked and your door
has been opened.
I have not been given a snake
but yet an egg,
that bursts its shell
and is born into
a world of flight,
and released from confines
into eternity.

263. Judgment Day

Lord,
Yours is justice, yours is mercy,
your commands balance the two,
on one hand the sorrow
of all our misses, wrong measures,
on the other you spare the innocent
among the multitudes of the guilty
who've yet to distinguish their thirsts,
their hungers, pleasures
from the commands of you.

You placed inside our spheres of thought
knowledge of ourselves in Eden,
a simple sampling knowing when doings done

have offended you, yet,
we go along, either ignoring you
or harboring our own crafted guilt,
until our eventual accountings,
when the judgment at judgment day is met.

264. All Your Finery

Maker of all,
If there is anything all your finery needs
more than the vitalizing sun,
it is the soaking, smoky rain that envelops
with fog and opaque distances made sure
through the fertile forest floor
where that which is not busy growing
is busy decomposing and needs your wet gift
as surely as the cactus needs the desert sun.

If there is anything your finery needs
it is your revolving hydrologic cycle
where the woods produce the lubricating logic
it requires for its survival,
a system feeding on itself
like a river flowing in a circle,
giving, taking, dispersing,
making up a whirlwind of rain, fog,
and vertical regeneration.

In the Smoky Mountains sometimes
it looks as if the sky is on the ground,
or that the mountains have no base
and are suspended in the heavens,
floating between grays, the color of ancient stone,
with foggy creeks rippling below.
This finery needs the vacant woods,
and its ample acres to be left alone.

265. I Am Serene

I am serene in my rest,
contented where the heart romps and reigns,
where the dark blood runs,
an internal river inside my chest.

I am serene even though
so many of my days have bloomed,
have come in peace to a crest soft as sand,
days with my forty year love,
a spouse who has become as familiar
as a limb, leg, hand.

I am serene even though
all the lovers of you who you beget,
are still menaced and have survived
Romans, pagans, tyrants all,
my time is in its eventual fall,
but it isn't winter yet.

I am serene because of you, Lord,
grateful to see, for the oxygen gift to be,
grateful for your blanketing, beckoning peace
that you gave to your disciples, prophets, saints, martyrs,
in the assurance that you gave
and have always given to all who say yes,
to them, to us, to me.

266. Intercede Now

Dark choice about, Holy Father,
the devil's on the perimeters,
he came this way weeks ago
and blew away a town,
now he comes in different form
as he always does, somehow,
but we've got you, Lord,
and I know that you
want us to do our own bidding,
but this time, please, intercede now.

267. Communion

Father,
We line up one by one
to touch you with our mouths,
to ingest your spirit food,
a wafer thin as paper,
the body of the Son.

We are all like new birds
just out of the egg,
on a limb with our beaks open,
waiting for your manna,
helpless as neophytes, hoping
to shepherd our humility.
We prepare for the time
when we will dine
with you in paradise.

The elders will all be there, then,
the ones we used to love and know.
We accept this promise of renewal, re-greening,
instead of dirt and death
being the ends of souls so that our lives now
look forward to your bliss,
or else lack meaning.

268. The Beauty

Lord,
Guide me through my passages without peril.
Save my children from the ravages that circumstance can bring.
Help me make my way straight to you.
Help me to show with hand what eye may see,
the beauty all around, above, below, beside me.
Allow your light to enter my eye and bounce back again
as an offering.
Continue to let me realize that frictions
are meant to tender our metal,
are meant to make us stronger and worthy of the gift of life.
Amen.

269. IN ANTITHESIS OF YOU

Lord,
Have we become a people
whose convenience and comfort,
whose favor for fitting in
shields us from acknowledging always present sin?
Have we become what you warned us about,
a people who edit your word,
excise the parts we dislike or fear,
hand pick those who do not
cause us conflict with the modern trends?
Are we like those who,
when confronted by Roman soldiers recanted
what they knew was true?
Are any of us ready to stand the test
that each generation is presented with,
a test that tries to lessen your word?
Father, round us up
so that we may stand together
against the onslaught that time
allows, in antithesis of you.

270. IN YOUR NAME

Lord,
In the Eternal City I prayed
for all those lost in your name,
beheaded, beguiled, beleaguered
from the crush of civilizations,
torched with flames of hate and fear,
secreted away yet not forgotten
in catacombs with your name
scribbled above their niches.

I pray now for all your word soldiers
tromping on through peril and resistance,
through ages rocked by storm and strife,
your troopers abiding by the guided life
martyred without mercy then and now,

to show us all that our sorrows in your name
have precedence in the ashes of ages.

271. Your Mosquitoes

Lord,
I know that you preside over infinite air, time
and finite earth and that flowing rivers,
distorted mountain pines, blind sea creatures and all
are not just of you,
but that I am none other than a mosquito on an elephant ear.

I saw another of your "mosquitoes" yesterday in the woods
after an afternoon rain.
A Luna moth was on the ground and flinching his tender wings
the way an infant's eyes squint at bright lights.
He was trying to open up and prepare for his moment,
the night, and make you proud of him.
I ask that you allow my children to open their green wings and fly
at their moments.
Amen.

272. Your Seal

Lord,
I have tried to wash my robe
and make it white in your blood.
I am begging for your seal
to be laced on my forehead,
and even though I am not worthy
to accept it,
I pray that I receive it.
I know that at times I falter
in my actions,
and there are many more deserving
of your grace placed
upon their heads,
still, I will continue to pray
for your approval, O Lord.
        From Revelations 7:2–4, 9–14

273. HOUSE WITHOUT WALLS

    Here I come, Lord,
    to a place no one has returned from,
    except you.
    I'm on the threshold, Lord,
    let it be wide.

    Should I not believe that
    beyond the terminal darkness there is light,
    how could I possibly go on?

    Should I not believe
    that on the other side of being now,
    this bliss of breath that you bestow,
    a river waits to take me
    in its currents to where
    all those who came before me
    and followed you know,
    and those who didn't, don't.

    Let me float the river's flow so I won't
    fail to flow into you, into them,
    for my welcome to your eternal
    house without walls.

274. I HAVE A NEW PAINTING

    Lord,
    I have a new painting
    and you're in it,
    not your physical substance
    or a picture of you
    but your unfailing luminous color,
    a suggestion of woods where winds sweep,
    placid water where your mirror is,
    the last murmur of small birds,
    dripping darkness, black rain,
    your silence promptly speaking,
    your surety softly keeping,
    flat and deep.

I have a new painting
with your voice gently waking,
the night in leaves and ground making,
your untarnished twirl of this the amber's fainting,
evening ensuing until the day
is only memory.

275. Glass Lives

Lord,
We are your children
and you are our father.
We cannot survive without you,
even though sometimes we think we can,
because we are both rational and irrational things,
the irrational often cannot be suppressed,
coerced, coached, persuaded or pleaded,
so keep us and guide us not to have
too much confidence in ourselves,
for history has proven we are not always noble, but needed,
are fallible and lead glass lives always liable to fracture
and there is no new method
that will produce different results,
other than you.

276. Man's Germ

Many have concocted potions
for the ills of man,
but man continues to be sick.
He spreads his flame with fire
in arts and sciences,
but it is not his flame that is ill,
but his wick.

Some have tried to hammer out faulty branches
with fist and boot,
but the hammerer's hand, his cure,
is not benevolent, not kind, lost of love,
is always worse than the disease,

is choking, wears brass knuckles, a chain mail glove.
It's not the branches of man in need
but the root.

Some have tried to strengthen man
by eliminating his weakest links
or corralling him into
a preferred box in order
to control how he thinks.

All of these medicines have at least once
had their unsuccessful turn,
they've come up empty, made things worse
in disinfecting man's germ.
He is and always has been
what you told us he was, O Lord,
man born with inevitable sin.

277. I Beg You, Go

Big yellow moon in my window,
coyote calls accompany it,
elsewhere, children suffer,
justice tilts to the dark side
of the scale without you, Lord,
in all black silence, punctuated by a pale glow
I pray to you, O Lord, to let it slow,
to ease the afflicted on this night,
in all their needs, I beg you, go.

10

October

278. If I Ever Get To Rome

If I ever get to Rome,
I'll walk the streets where,
in centuries past those who believed in you
walked, cried, were persecuted and died,
with great pathos and a heart of pity,
I will feel like I am home,
and in the place of your sons Peter and Paul,
whose chains still hang in a church
in the Eternal City.

If I ever get to Rome,
I will walk the Via Appia
and think of Peter supposedly seeing you there
and asking "Domine, quo vadis?"
and I will ask the same,
Lord, where are you going?
Go with me and keep my faith
the way those so long ago kept theirs.

279. Fishing

I wish that I could go
to waters where the fish are jumping,
anticipation romping, heart thumping,
a take a day at the lake day
with panoramic calm,

quiet, daybreak balm in silvery blue,
far from any weary way
like your disciples, Lord,
who fished not just for food to eat,
but for another kind, to fish for you.

But you have made the fish wily
as you have hidden your stewardship of all,
we never know when they will bite,
you've the same workings for all of us,
for fishers of fish and men,
magical, indeterminable, sustainable,
and for our knowledge, forbidden,
for should we know when the fish would bite
or the whens and hows of your ways,
we would not want to fish, or believe.

280. Here the Reason Born

Lord,
Here the triumph of days,
at least mine but not all others,
here the joy of your love
for me and all my brothers,
even those who deny you.

Here the reign of grateful breath,
the oxygen engine propelling,
here comforting evidence
of your grace compelling
to all, there through two millennia.

For what else is there
that gives the peace of flowers,
that can be ours?
Here the reason born
for seasons past the grave.

281. I Promise To Do Better

Lord,
Shame on me
for breaking my conduct code, and more,
in dalliances of unholy passages,
when I wander, weave or stray
away from your suggested way,
in deeds done or not,
in actions you would deplore.

Forgive me, Lord,
I am only one weak will,
I try my best but still
lean away from the Word, spirit, and letter
to what you suggest we listen,
to your quiet voice
in the night the whippoorwill,
I promise, Lord, to do better.

282. Let It Be Alone

In the dark, Lord,
the skies electrifying in the west,
the storm is on its way
and all any of us can do is pray
that it misses us in its wrath,
its path where it can do
whatever it chooses,
and whenever the wrath arrives
everyone loses,
so should there be a storm, Lord,
let it be in pastures where
even cows have escaped,
let it be alone.

283. Pleased With My Gnosis

Lord,
I am not afraid with you
in struggles, rifts, losses,
a monster knocks at my door
and I know what to do.

In strains and minuses,
peace taken from dreary days
that used to be granted given,
I navigate perilous water,
wait and trust in your ways.

Deliver me, O Lord,
to a pleasant prognosis,
past the vermin infested present,
past birdless silence of lost innocence,
I'm pleased with my gnosis.

284. Time for the Poets

No more days like this, O Lord,
ways with deer on lawns,
sun yellow rain hiss
after a drought the sky's silver kiss,
desires of mouths and would-be leaves.
You and me at the pinnacle of passages, not streets,
ceaseless tug of sensing growth around,
rejoicing blooms, cardinal eggs,
but some streets elsewhere cruel, unforgiving,
rustlers of sorrow command the ground,
blood stained sidewalks, children compromised,
we're not there but
in the woods, rejoicing, living.

The circle of is and was
is with a faulty flat tire,
the good do their best
though it's not enough,

time now for poets to get tough
and for the tough to be poets.

Progress toward dissolution's
not a favorable direction
but a defeating choice,
it's time for the poet's insurrection,
Bastille-storming battering ram voice
setting beauty free
from its current word lords,
we're in the woods, doubting not,
you and me.

285. Glorious Day

Lord,
He staggers through his days
broadsided by a whack upside the head,
a monstrous event of unfathomable ill,
he walks but does not run,
he wonders how to go on,
no shade, no peace, only searing sun
in hopeless hours that drag along,
in grueling days without his son,
O Lord if he can see
that your father gave the gift of resurrection
to him, to us, to me,
and some day, some sweet day
he will be there with his son
as you are with your father
and what a glorious day that will be.

286. In Your Hand

Father,
You are the sparkplug of seed,
the tender that bolts bud from branch,
the juice that cracks the soil with new growth.

What else could account for the burst
of life from lifelessness,
heat from hibernation,
movement from stillness,
somethingness from nothingness?

Father, you are all around us
and yet we see you not,
we see the flame but what
enables it is subtle, and hot.
Allow us a different kind of vision
so that we may see
the force that is in your hand
surround us.

287. Happy Paleolithic Cave

Father,
The skeptics do not see
salvation signs for your followers,
they do not see
any connection between your believers
and good fortune
and do not acknowledge
that Satan is on the field
of play every day scoring points,
keeping the ball away from you,
they do not realize that sometimes you take
in order to make
something better, stronger,
or that all our suffering is not for naught.
The skeptics doubt, dismiss,
or ignore you for this,
when they ought to know that should we
all be forever accommodated by pleasing fate,
we'd have no reason ever for your son to save
us from our own satisfactions
and would all be living peacefully,
ignorantly, without progress, curiosity or destiny,
without quests, resurgences, or growth,
in some happy Paleolithic cave.

288. Stand By Me

Lord, You have always stood by me,
coming to my rescue and saving me
from peril, allowing me to escape under the fence
when some beside me did not.

I remember them all,
all those times you helped
without fanfare, without being obvious,
behind the scenes with your grace,
and I knew it then and praise you now
for all those times.

Lord, Please don't abandon me,
allow me to carry on, at least for awhile,
to see my grandbabies grow to
whatever they are destined
by you to be.
Lord, allow me to be too
and wrap me in your hands.
Amen.

289. The Hummingbirds Are Gone

Father,
Thank you for those little
buzzing signposts,
that tell us a season is upon us,
thank you for letting us see
the tiny ruby throated birds about.

But the hummingbirds are gone,
their territorial battles have passed,
their darting and mid-air struggles
with one of their kind
on a flowered bush or feeder.

They arrive in spring
after the frost has been forgotten,
their coming signals sunny days ahead

and summer dense drapery of the woods
and in their goings
they take with them their miniature
winged bit of you, O Lord.

290. War and Peace

Lord, the world continues wrestling with war
and only when the wrestlers rest
do we have brief periods of peace.
Mobs build their hatreds the way
winds build storms in seas,
first with small antagonisms,
then into swells of destruction
and as long as there are winds and ways
it will be so.

Father, will we all have to wait until
you come for there to be order, justice, love?
Will these children of the earth ever grow up?
Do we, should we, console ourselves
to be prepared for war but pray for peace?
Help us, father, toward the latter.

291. Identifiable Posts

Lord, we said so much
but wished we had said more.
Somehow in all the talk
we forgot to tell him
how proud we were of him.

He and his sister are heart-most,
paramount in the amount
of love and ever well wishing, praying,
that we bestow upon them, a fount
that bids them well,
they are marks upon the skin of the living,
identifiable posts.

Does the dove's love of its eggs give
a sadness in its coo?
At early mornings or days' endings,
it weeps for its eggs' departures,
in the live oaks, in the pines, fields,
it weeps for its children,
and for you,
O Lord.

292. THE THIRD EYE

Father,
You gave us a third eye
that sees what is not shown,
that sees the open door
of cages where doves have flown,
free but still susceptible
to actions you deplore,
an eye that sees past
deceivers present in all the days
who bare false witness without pause,
who recruit others to their sordid ways.

We see them, Lord,
but only if we use your hidden gifts and instead
of joining herds running toward cliffs,
we detect wrongness from the heart
and not the head.

293. QUENCH THE ARROW

Father,
Quench the arrow
that always flies
to each of us
at least once if not more.

Provide a balm
for the blistering breath
of longevity that rips
the red heart's ventricle.

Calm the currents that wash
us away to where we should not be.
Sooth the ulcerous ages of anger
that propel armies to embark.

Lift us to where we sail above,
in skies of heaven before death
and watch the misbehavings
of those who know you not.

294. For You, For This, for That

Lord,
I pray for the weak,
for those with hardened hearts,
for those who deny and do not see
the bud, bloom, tide, the sea,
the complex workings of ordinary life
all around, everywhere, the arrangements
all too detailed to have arrived
at their integrated harmony by themselves,
I think,
for winds that prune the trees,
for winter frost that dispenses insects
lest they get out of control,
for the rains, to the weeds a drink,
for the infants, their tender eyes
not yet set for sight,
for spouses co-existing in happy habitat,
for children who grow slowly
into their own right,
for all the above, Lord,
for you, for this, for that.

295. I Am the Hand

Lord,
I am the hurting, helping hand,
the hand that searches, reaches out,
that fumbles, falls, records, points, paints,
that shakes, salutes heroes,

the hand that pays my tithe,
that puts itself on shoulders
of the saints,
that shakes in fear
not from your enemies but from their doings,
that opens itself to your eternal love.
I am the hand,
you are the glove.

296. Songbirds, Coyotes, and Us

Father of all,
does the songbird sing his song
as surroundings celebration,
or does he sing because
his close feathered mate is gone?
Do our music makers drone
about missing or gone lovers,
or do they make the ones they love leave,
all for the sake of droning?

Just who do coyotes howl to?
Is it you, Lord,
the eponymous ear of all?
Should we have your ear,
you should have ours,
hearing prayers of songbirds,
coyotes and us.

297. Forgive Me Lord

Lord,
Forgive us for the arrogance of our age,
that so many think they can go
on today and future days without you.
So many of us are like Narcissus
and have fallen in love
with reflections of ourselves,
and think that with our mighty minds
that you gave to us,
just as you gave the gazelle its speed,

the eagle his superior sight and flight,
so we use our one tool
to play the fool
and insist that we have no need
of your other gifts and that we are right.
Forgive us Lord,
for not being worthy of you.

298. I Imbibe in Your Offerings

I imbibe in your offerings, Lord,
of silhouetted evenings
along the freeway toward home,
with all the others on their way
somewhere safe inside their cars,
talking on cell phones
or listening to music,
making the miles anonymous.

Even the music is an offering,
as is the big sky putting on a show.
Here in the remains of a day
you have decided to make yourself known
and I know.

I know it's you, hardly ever seen
in yellow wind in tall Kansas grasses
or blue, white capped waves
far from any ever watchful eye.
You sneak in now and then,
and those who refuse to acknowledge you
are only perpetuating the never dying lie.

Lord, feel free to show yourself to me
at any time, I promise,
I'll stop what I am doing,
enjoy, and imbibe.

299. Endowed by Our Creator, You

Lord,
You set down a code long ago
that has proved to be a harness
for the excesses we are heir to,
without it we cast adrift,
subject to our own ad-lib law,
capable of justifying anything
because, without you
there are no boundaries.

I am grateful, Lord,
that you provided the light and wisdom
to our forefathers who based their law
on you, that all are created equal,
without which, without boundaries
we eat our own, but with them,
we are endowed by our creator, you.

300. O, John

O John,
You were the youngest of the bunch,
there beside our Lord at the supper
and the very end but somehow
you had your adolescent hunch
to follow and you did all the way
to a cave at Patmos where,
hiding from Domition
on scrolls you wrote like no other
in spirit contraband
your revelations
in a godly trance so that now
we are still trying to understand.

301. Pas de Deux

Lord of nature,
two wrens do their pas de deux
on my porch with much ado,

bobbing, bobbing, weaving up and down
and are not happy
that I am here, around
their little nest with baby chicks,
waiting for their grubs.

They are like all the other
spring birds in the woods filling
your orchestrated music here and now.
I'm a spectator willing
to be quiet and not disturb the mother
as she flutters with wren worry,
not yet knowing that I am not the enemy,
instead, enjoying my front row seat
with cyclical new life living,
energetic, charged, thrilling.

302. The Tanager Is My Manager

The tanager manages
the end of day animal buzz,
my evenings when the wind is tiring,
were he not here
I'd have to conscript him in his red rendering
as an hireling
and pay him to do what he does.

He comes when all the other birds
have gone on to roost,
my crimson bugler bugling
amongst pines and sweetgums
he comes again and again to boost
the day's retiring,
dunks himself into birdbath splendor,
flies like a bottle rocket
and tonight is driven away by the rain.

303. A Platform Built

Lord,
Should we remember where we've been
to know where we are going?
Should we wipe the chalkboard clean,
throw our oars overboard
and cease our old rowing?

Should we believe we are susceptible
to foibles ancient old,
think we are exempt from sin,
begin anew, without you,
in hopes long tried, stale, over sold?

Should we not ask
what brought us to our current fold,
a platform built through centuries
of martyrs, selfless souls,
or hide behind our imprinted mask?

304. Grateful for My Journey

Lord,
It is difficult for many
to understand that you know all,
that you know the numbers of leaves on trees,
the quantity of shells in seas,
birds on wings, bloomings in springs,
but not for me.

I know that I am fearfully,
wonderfully made by you,
that I rose from my father's seed to reach
into what I have become now,
and know that you know
when I sit or stand, sleep, or eat a peach,
my fears, my every need.

I am thankful for my journey,
from thence my mother's womb,
am grateful for every day
I have been awarded,
for yesterday, today and until
I am laid into my resting terminal tomb.

305. You Have the Key

Lord,
The dirt is a trap
and it can be shut,
the earth is a door
and it can be locked.
We have an allotted time to be
and after our days
which we have measured, treasured, stocked,
have ceased, only you
can unlock the door.
Only you have the key.

We will be lifted, escorted
as you were, again, shall we,
to a new life without unwelcome toil,
escorted from the wormy soil
to new life.
You have the key.

306. The Edge at First Chorus

Father,
At the early edge the source delivers
with blazing blades of light
that cut cool fog
like a knife into a yellow melon.
At that moment, with beacons broken by trees,
with beams that scatter through the woods
like headlights on a rainy road
with sun streams that bring birdsong
into an echoed chorus,

that bring crow caws and squirrels
performing monkey tricks in trees,
I watch the woods, your woods, awake.

307. My Signals

Lord,
Sailboat mast past the reefs, closer to shore,
I'm in the crow's nest looking for you.
Should I run aground?
Should I not expect
for you to show
the way you have before?

I'm looking but have noticed
you always show when I'm not,
when I am driving,
crossing a bridge over a muddy river,
or the time you showed up
as a puppy dog in the road,
or as you did at Fort Sam Houston when you let the rain
fall in my face and wash my fear away,
or the way you did
when you were the wind
and visited my ear?

So now, Lord, I beg you
to visit those who
are in need of a hint of your presence,
a burning bush, a flicker in an inattentive eye,
for those who need you at this hour
more than me.

308. Restoration

There is a wholeness ever lessening,
when those we love depart from us
for a new destination,
a hole is left that needs filling,
an empty yearning,

a will slowed and not yet willing
to abandon memory of times together,
we feel alone and wait
for you to give us peace, Lord,
and restoration.

11

November

309. Not Endless Rivers

Lord,
Blindness would not be best
even if we were all blind
because the eye is made to see the way
a leg is for walking, a tongue for tasting,
a nose for a rose, blue to a jay.

There are apples we can see
whose carts should be upright,
surely so, lest we quiver
on an unmoored vessel with nothing stationary,
no sacrament, no sanctity,
with all our wisdoms eternally suspect
and thus no wisdom at all,
only riverboat chatter on an endless black river.

No, our rivers are not endless
but wash and sway with prayers and pleas,
and keep us above currents
that threaten carts and horses,
cats, pigeons, mountains, minions, marshes,
and ours, no matter how long or brief,
are emptied into eternal seas.

310. Saint Francis

Saint Francis, I have revered nature as did you
and know the tangled tonic of essence so complete,
even at its smallest denomination detailed
that it was made and wrought by the one we both love.
I ask that I may be more like you
and that the Lord we share runs ahead of me,
blocking the venoms of circumstance,
snakes in the way, serpents of certainty,
especially for my family,
so that they may run beside me, kicking up dust of decades
toward the ends of the earth,
towards the airless time when
the rhythm of the lungs is silent,
towards grace best demonstrated by you in your sacrificial life.

311. The Maestro of Majestic Cohesion

Father, You are the maestro of majestic cohesion,
at daybreak your grand schematic
comes into view, now,
and dirty sand colored deer
slide stealthily through the woods,
smooth as otters over waters not far from here.

You are the maestro who conducts, instructs,
blows the precious bubble of be,
that has its limits,
its thin walls fragile
to ruptures of sin, calamity.

You are the maestro who
recycles seasons through their changes
here in the piney woods,
through swamps and seas,
prairies and great mountain ranges.
You are the thorn in the shoe of stasis.
I watch as the summer season undresses.

312. Rest Across the River

Father, take us farther forward
and protect us from uselessness.
Save us from weakness,
from the new that has lost its finish,
from aged clinging and infant fragility,
in the lingering light and long night.
Make our allotment expansive,
our fears vanquished,
our faith rewarded with your love,
from you, eternal giver,
until it is our time
and we can rest across the river.

313. Lord,

Some are still hanging on now,
glowing orange and yellow,
drifting down like colored snowflakes
in the fall wind that whips the hardwoods
of their dressings.

One by one they reach the ground
and turn to dust that feeds the soil
that feeds the trees
that feeds the air,
all and all around
in an everlasting cycle.

Soon they will be no more,
with winter in the branches stripped bare,
your divine work over again,
just like last year and the years before,
stealing summer of its green
in an eternal circumference of seasons,
now and forever.

314. I Will Be Rich

O Lord,
You replenish the cups of those
who use you as a convenience,
they speak your name yet you
are absent in their hearts
as evidenced by their deeds,
they ignore, even defy you
and wear "pride as their necklace",
they do not do your work but tint the stream of life
with acrid color,
they secure dominion over others
and seek to make them submissive,
they prosper in youth, die old,
while your sheep perish in righteousness,
they boast and are self served, assured,
so convinced are they that they are right,
yet in spite of a lofty niche,
I choose you and your promise
and after we are both terra interred,
I'm the one who will be rich.
        From Psalms 73:6

315. Satan's Seed

Lord Jesus, Satan's seed sprouts
a kernel of a tumor never wanted,
inside ourselves and those we love,
unlike your seeds which bring
life to creatures that bloom and grow,
his brings cellular malfeasance
and sometimes death to your creations.

We all want to know
how to battle his champion seed
that unlike your bean brings no food,
no flower nectar, no fetal promise,
his brings a victory stewing
with errant expansions within

and is a triumph on or under the skin
not of your doing.
Lord, show your hand,
don't let him win.

316. Plentitude

Lord,
You have taken from me some of my greatest treasures
yet you have given so much more.
You have given me with each inhalation the be-all breath,
the ability to see plentitude's measure.
You have given me sight blessings
valued above all, for pleasure.
I am not asking that you now give me special favors,
only that you do not hinder me with circumstance
and that you let me go my way.
I will try to make myself worthy of your abundance,
I will not take anything for granted.
If given the opportunity,
I will spend my time trying to make others
more aware of the beauty and grace
common as termites, plankton, and ants
that exist under every leaf and salty sea,
pasture, plain, forest, desert and field.
Please help me make my own offering.

317. Perennial Protein Truth

There is a benevolent largesse ever more,
a gentle host among us,
there for the taking should we ask,
that is as internal as an implanted tooth,
that settles on the hillsides like a Jell-O flood,
that is a gelatin thick wave that covers most,
the perennial protein truth
of you, O Lord.

318. I Salute the Son and Sun

Lips in petals,
our medals for seeing,
eyes in water, or was it a mirror?
Voice in wind
and we know whose,
mystery in fire that cooks the muse.
I salute joy in doings done,
the chicken in my pot,
days allotted for my run.

Darkness approaching,
dimming sight,
in the muddy purple evening
I salute vestiges of the sun,
and when leaves are lost in black
as you did once in light,
you come back,
and I salute the night and you, the son.

319. Face to Face

When the light from this porch darkens,
extinguished like a lit match
to never strike again,
and from here the rains
on metal roofs go unheard,
this western wind has done its run,
let no one mourn the loss,
considering all the gains, gifts, and grace,
when I meet you, Maker,
face to face.

320. I Will Proceed

Lord,
I take a hit, the wound is deep
but not too deep,
I've wandered off now to sleep
and dreamed that you saved me,
again,

as you have so many times before,
just as I bruise, bleed,
step closer to the one-way door
that leads from this life,
you pull me back again
as I ask what need
have you of me.
Show me, Lord, and I will proceed.

321. The Potential of Smooth

I believe in the potential of smooth,
it has been and can be, all,
should we rid ourselves
of man made woe and its architects,
and rejoice in a voice
of virgin violins crying over cypress arms,
and the potential of smooth
asserts itself as the choice
that you would have us make,
O Lord.

322. Speak To Me

Lord,
You were there when Henry IV
knelt in the snow,
in the snow too at Valley Forge,
but those who disavow you ask
where you were at Verdun, Normandy, Antietam,
and ask why you hide your face.
Those of us who avow know
that should you be readily visible to us,
what need would there be for grace,
what wages spent for faith?

Should you be easily seen,
what effort would be needed
to separate those who believe
from those who merely say the words?

You're there for us in camouflage,
nestled amongst the weeds,
in angel's wings that flap in silence,
undetected from the unfaithful ear,
there for all to hear with weary need
who gather with more than insurance
that to not gather would bring them fear.

Father, speak to me in your own sign
that I may learn to listen,
that I may learn to wear
that faith that guides us through
years of times
when we think that you're not there.

323. Show Me the Way

Lord,
Show me the way,
should I stumble will I know
I am headed wrongly?
Should I prosper will I know
the opposite?
Do you regularly intervene
in the affairs of men and women,
or only on a larger scale
when you manage to turn the tide
of history the way you want it turned?
Are we of such conceit that we think
you decide our every move,
or are we wrong to think otherwise?
How free are wills and designed dividends,
how planned shows, midterms, ends?
When do we know we know?
Lord, show me the way and I will follow.

324. Not By Chance

Father,
None are so blind
as those who refuse to see,
none so deaf
as those who do not listen
to what your son has to say.

You send out messages to us
in divine numbers,
written in codes we must discover,
in Fibonacci sequences of growth,
in golden sections of design components
arrayed before us if we choose
to see them, if we join the geometry dance
and notice that all that is before us
did not arrive and happen here by chance.

325. Reliance on Signs

You took Thomas to task,
showing us again your essence,
that he should have to ask
for a sign, when signs are for
the weak in faith in your presence,
although still come to us
when we least expect them,
lest we rely on them for our proof,
which is and should not be
a reason for us to believe in you,
O Lord.

Pilate, the Sanhedrin and others
asked why you did not save yourself
on the cross, but you knew better
than to be obvious in your day,
for obviousness obscures faith
so that who would know true
believers from followers
of an easy, unsubstantiated way.
          From John 20:29

326. Por Favor, El Senor

I've had enough of tenacious pathogens
beehiving in the red stream,
of rusty joints, creaky bones,
arches flat on a cold floor,
of the degenerative march
with me as drum major,
so, come to my aid,
por favor, El Senor.

I've had enough of the eternal vigilance
from the enemies of you,
O El Senor,
that poison wells of speech,
skewer history already made
so they may control the future.
It is to you I beseech,
come to my aid, our aid,
por favor, El Senor.

327. Did You Mean?

Lord,
Did you mean that we should be
like the lilies of the field,
and surrender our fate
to the same pulse that swells
the silent seed to bloom,
that generates the flower,
that pulse that has always been
the breath and rhythm of your Father?

Did you mean that we should
take no heed to any needs
but trust that it will be met,
yet not be asleep and fail to forge ahead
with fruits, pursuits
of our own passions, seeds, deeds,
as long as we pursue them
not for our own selves but for others?

Did you mean
that we pick up our crosses, today or tomorrow
and follow you, knowing that whatever
happens, happens without our understanding,
unless there is something better than this,
this brief bliss interrupted by sorrow?

Did you mean that without suffering
we cannot get close to you?
Should we see our losses
as earthly semi-scourgings that never cease,
our badges of testimony too
and that there is only real justice, real peace,
when we escape our mortal boundaries
and come to you?
        From Matthew 5:3–10

328. Thanksgiving Prayer

Father,
How can I begin
my feeble thanks of blessings now,
should I start with breath itself,
the precious privilege of the living
you set into us at our birth, then,
the endowed instinct to ventilate
even though no one showed us how?

Should I include too the family
that is always there in thoughts and deeds,
especially the children, our future's seeds,
include too this country of my kin,
where we possess so many of the things
that filled our father's dreams?

Should I include the blessings of sight,
as many as the leaves,
parched gold, red and orange in the fall,
the wind across the lake,

releasing a strand of hair
across her forehead, announcing,
confirming, representing is-ness,
this life for all, for your sake?

329. Thanks for Giving

Lord,
Thank you for a lifetime of sights,
of times, friends, remembered moments, lovers,
episodes, enemies,
forever fulfilling gifts,
for green tea,
for wine that is art,
toadstools, cocoons that burst into wings,
for the wind on the lea,
leaf ripping storms, winter rain,
salty eternal sea,
the blood of our non-aquatic lives,
your Godly made things.
Thanks for giving
the whole wonderment of
a gleaming, grateful eye.

330. Embellishments

Lord,
We go no where
when we stray from you,
the winds still blow, tides change,
all the organics breathe, grow and die,
you make your own embellishments, these,
but when we make ours absent of you
we go no where,
even though we think we do.

Those in history who rose,
their embellishments grand and known,
who soared in stature without you
and mostly did more harm then good,

not knowing that to assume the reins of many
one must bow to something greater than himself
lest he live without knowing his limits,
what people in cars on freeways,
roofers on housetops, workers in fields,
wish he or she would do.

I come to you today
in your house of prayer,
as those others of you
and in you have come
through two millennia,
to thank you for your ultimate gift
of meaning and the seed
you planted in me long ago
and I pray for those who deny you
for their final day will be a sad one,
indeed.

331. A New Start

Lord,
Like your father,
he lost his only son,
his trials have now begun
and he will have to live
with an abscess in his heart,
a deep abrasion slow to heal,
a son gone whose love he can feel
and he needs you now, Lord,
to intercede and show him the way
to you, so he can make a new start.

332. I Am Only Me

Lord,
You alone can cure my ills,
can answer my prayers,
can save me from any raging storm,
intercede into my affairs,
but why should you?

I am only me,
a tiny seed among the granaries
of the fertile earth,
a water drop in the windy sea,
and only one of your minions
among your millions.

I am only me,
so why should you single me out,
when others request your hand
with more needs than mine?
But I can hope,
and I can pray,
and wait for the answer
that comes from none but thee.

333. Perpetual Motion

Always on my way from hither to yon,
moving, knowing, always going,
a moving actionary,
not content with stasis,
eschewing "now" for "there".

Few places are found
that justify immobility,
I'm walking with humility
along a free form trail.
Sometimes the scent's undetectable
but then I offer an audible
that could be heard by any hound.

I'm roam ready,
ready for Rome or San Miguel,
an eco trip from San Juan,
not running from but to,
except the distancing time allows
for those past, their shadows on me
like a sycamore's on a lawn.

I'm in voyage forward from right here,
from this moment to tomorrow's,
have dodged rattlers on the path so far,
even now, their tails wiggle near,
content to be any place,
especially when you are there.

334. Reason for Righteousness

Lord, are we to believe
that we were left here all alone,
that for the faith we all had,
the blessings we all sought,
that all our cries, prayers
from all the centuries
were all for naught?

Should I believe that,
what reason would there be
to continue, and by what authority
would there be for any purpose
for righteousness?
No, should that be true,
then we are all in a free-for-all
with every man and woman for himself, herself,
with every person's only motive
being self-service.

335. Will This Be the Last?

I always wondered every time we left her
and she would be standing on her porch waving goodbye,
would this be the last time to see her?
And then one day when not wondering, it was.

I always wondered every time we left our house,
would this be the last time to see it?
Would some storm, fire, fallen tree
or some other calamity take it from us
in our absence?

I always wondered every time we kissed and parted,
would this be the last kiss?
Wondered when we said goodbye to our children
if we would see them again,
and now, Lord, I wonder
every time I leave your house,
with church bells ringing,
will this be the last?

336. A Perilous Future

Lord, I remember the day
when I was standing with a brigade of men
waiting for my military orders,
Viet Nam, now, later, or when?
We were in formation, five hundred strong.
Moments before my fate arrived,
I looked upward and rain began to fall
slowly into my face
and I knew that it was your tears
for all the men who would race
off to fight in remote jungles.
My orders came and I was one of the few
spared such a future.

Today, the rain was falling again
on my way to receive my biopsy report
and this time, the tears were for me.
I knew then and now
that you are with me
on my journey into a perilous future, Amen.

337. Honey In The Ears

Lord,
You gave us a songbird in our throats
that sings no matter what,
that sings in times of good,
in times of woe and is not
ever going to stop.

O music, the butter of the muse,
the blood is jumping,
the heart thumping and dancing
like a one-legged man in spring.

A violin in a room
or trumpet in the fields
is honey in the ears,
a sweet and sure remedy for silence.

So let the strings, reeds, pipes and percussions play on,
for what the rose is to the nose
and breaking light to the eye,
so is the rhythm that sounds the way a feeling feels.

338. In Your Lap

Lord,
Thank you for our little enclave
we carved out of thick nothings,
of intrusive vines that once choked it.
Thank you for lush evidence
of your magnetic, static pulse
that beats silently,
except when a frog, cricket or bird
lets their voices be heard.

Thank you for our sanctuary,
mostly safe from public poison,
shielded by weeds and blooms,
that lets us sit here, within
and feel the pulse that is rain, wind,
intricate bio-kingdom exposed,
bugs, birds, earth, sap,
you are here and we
are in your lap.

339. No Other Reason

There is no other reason
for the planets to orbit the sun
or the electrons, atoms, wet pea seed
to swell, sprout and bloom
into a new pea bush,
no other reason for the embryo
with its beak to crack the egg
and enter into the world outside,
for drumming hearts in breasts to reside,
for the changing of leaf colors
from yellow green to green
to orange to red to brown,
for the womb of the earth, uterine seas
deep as mountains are high,
harboring all its varied fishes and their wishes,
no other reason for all these demonstrations
than your hand at the tiller
in all your orchestrations,
O Lord.

340. Just Another

Lord,
Allow me just another fall
to split the firewood with my axe,
when frost burnt leaves flutter horizontally
beneath baby blue skies,
allow me just another winter
when white wraps the gravy-brown woods
and creatures leave their tracks
giving away their whereabouts,
allow me just another spring
when the resurrection cycle begins again
on which the promise of the egg relies,
allow me just another summer
with warm water gravel bar swimming,
the memory of cool nights dimming,
allow me just another decade

with my image and my lover's
still in the mirror,
then another, O Lord, just another.

341. No Idea

They probably sat out on porches
on Palatine Hill and watched the sun set
over the not yet crumbled Forum Romanum,
and wondered who this guy was,
this guy, you, Lord,
who promised to free not all slaves
but all from the slavery of death.

They didn't see it coming, Lord,
when they destroyed the Jerusalem temple,
felt victorious and built Titus' arch
with menorahs chiseled high within the curve,
prancing horses with now missing legs
just above eye level.
The arch rose high above the forum
that now lies in ruins in the sun.
They had no idea, Lord,
what they had done.

12

December

342. O Winter

O winter, where have you been?
All of a sudden, you show up,
the snow turns to sleet, then rain,
then to snow again.

O winter, how long will you stay?
The creatures have already had enough
standing in wet fields freezing, ice coated,
searching desperately for food,
pine warblers gathering,
a convention of little feathery green,
and only the ducks are happy.
Lord, we want for this to fade,
for you to usher in
your majestic azalea spring.

343. Launching

There beneath golden boughs and leaves of recurrent rust
a prayer is launched to you, O Lord, bathed in soluble shade,
trusting that beyond the trees a pale pure draft of diesel-strong will
waits to turn wind from the lea
and instead in response to giving, give to me.

In summer's spoiled fields winds are cold across the lake,
in evenings without rain or art, the torso percussion heart
fills with wonder, worries,

leaves fall like ash that still holds its fire,
the wind brings rain, the forecast: flurries.

Launching an indoor prayer day,
the fireplace light paints
an empty teacup gold,
coffee black as burnt oil is on its way.
It will get better, warmer,
or at least that's what we are told.

Waiting out the bristling breeze with geese in v's overhead,
masters of a higher blue on their warmer waters way,
below, wishes for pumpkin orange, dirty brown, weather fair,
burnt out grasses, sickly fields above worried waters,
the sun gray-veiled, concealed in memory,
the voice is lost but not the prayer.

344. Electronic Drug

Dependent more and more on an electronic drug
that shoots its wad at the speed of light,
our youth are encased, Lord,
in a tomb of chatter that might
deliver them outside the gates
of social discourse,
far and away from face to face parlance,
away from surely showing up,
away from minds that grow
as their bodies do,
that expands from real presence and touch,
away from that most necessary source,
that is you, O Lord.

345. Our Disabled Propositions

On Mt. Olympus they turned over rocks,
keys were found that unlocked doors to marble men,
to the beauty baton passing, to the classical nose,
to Lady Samothrace with puffed wings,
Madonna lips in oil, frescoes of you, Lord,

lost arms, glowing Frederick Church icebergs,
to Pre-Raphaelite hair, black Rodin flesh in stone,
a long run of ancestral blessing,
the best of propositions now alone,
to go forward.

And so our disabled propositions
are buried in banal dribble,
great drawings reduced to scribble,
stone chiseled into nothing but stone,
paint without spark,
buildings into dead walls,
ghosts of spatial spirits in the dark,
only white enclosures for the lonely.

Dismissed before but returning,
new again, reaffirming
the eye and tongue's dominion over the head,
inextinguishable firey light, rubber jewel
bouncing, ever yearning,
for spirit shadow, glorious structure,
water, wine, fuel.

346. Put Me on Your Prayer List

Lord Jesus,
Do you pray to your father for us?
If so, keep me in mind until I'm through.
You and your father and the spirit are three in one,
so keep me kept in safety,
could you?

Either we are no more important than rats
or you have infused us
with a subcutaneous spirit
which some mistake for mind,
because of that gift you gave
we have awareness of ourselves and others,
it follows us to the grave, in kind.

We can use it for stupendous strides
and sometimes we think we accomplish them alone,
we ride the air, the earth, the tides,
speak and see electronically across miles,
we've made quite a name for ourselves
but it's the jewel you gave us that we own.

Lord,
all three of you do not pray
but are the ears of prayer,
hearing us through the noise, dark, mist,
hearing us when we don't even speak,
hearing, taking us at your appointed hour.
Lord, if by chance you do pray,
put me on your prayer list.

347. Your Vine

Lord,
We are the branches of your vine,
yet some of us bear fruit,
some not,
some bear poisonous fruit,
some none,
some render fruit that is sweet
to the mouths of the needy,
that gives love and hope
to a love starved world,
some render fruit that benefits
only themselves in their quests
for things not of you,
that bear money, fame, or power
and in the quiet hour
that others save for your bread and blood,
they are not to be heard,
they have listened but not to your word
that promises the fruit of unending life.

348. The Baroque

Father, I must admit that I
have taken a likening to the Baroque,
a conversion that even though
I do not appreciate any less yet,
the smooth simple styling
of a sure, common set,
I've taken to the curl, the lavishly carved,
the intricate, layered,
struggled upon compilations,
that so often have been made
as tributes to you,
in image, song and stone,
I take on these treasures
in full and flattering tone.

349. An In Between

There is an in between
last light and first dark,
an in between summer's ending,
fall's beginning,
king snake's sweetness
and cobra anger,
between sound fading away slowly
until it is no longer heard
and a bugle shortly away from its source.

There is an in between too,
you and us, Lord,
and the way we choose to go.
Sometimes we come and are here,
sometimes we go and are with you,
should we decide to make it so.

350. The Red Shouldered Hawk is Blessed Also

Father, the red shouldered hawk adorns my eyes
in my yard, and he chooses the days.

I watch him and am thankful for him
and know that he knows the plan,
that he is to stay awake and use his wits
you gave him so that he could
fit into the plan, your plan.

He chooses the days to sit in my pine
by the lake's morning edge,
usually after a rain
when the crawfish crawl out of the water
and threaten to spontaneously evolve
into earthly creatures;
it is then that the hawk's eye sees one
and catches it, then sits proudly
on my blue bird house to dine.
The next day I see pre-owned
red crawfish pinchers drying in the sun,
their reds and oranges leaving them,
bleached by light, their shells shine.

351. Some Seek the Sours

Father,
We could partake of the fruits that are yours in love
but instead some swallow the sours that are ours.
We could embrace peace, joy,
instead some seek the sours if they choose.
We could show patience, generosity, gentleness, self control,
instead some seek the sours,
that germinate in their hearts and eyes,
and over time take their toll,
these choices that go rancid
in the days of days' demise.
Instead, some seek the sweet serene,
parsing peace with each new breath
with no more sours but honey days with you, Lord,
for there has already been enough death.

352. Just What We Are Capable Of

There have been those who took inordinate share
of your gifts, Lord, and we are the better from it,
the almost dead ears of Beethoven gave us his
inner sound, his supplemental tones,
and the tortured Vincent in his coloring book rooms,
who had a fire that extinguished itself.
We have gift taker Hildegard and her chants,
Bach's church music for the soul,
they all took their shares and shared
and we are better from it.

Lord,
You allow the good, the great,
and then seldomly but always on time,
the extraordinaries who show us
just what we are capable of.

353. The Founding Fathers

Lord Jesus,
They were right in their view
that providence would be forthcoming
for those who followed you,
maybe not today, right now, or tomorrow
but over the ages a lessening of sorrow
for the masses
but as time passes,
foolishness comes and goes
and you provide the possibilities
for prosperity, should it not be stolen
by those with no allegiances
save their own squalid results
that are there to be seen,
through a tortured Godless history.

354. New Arcadia

Father,
I ran in haste across a line
between faith and disinterest
and found you,
who were always there
like the light behind my back
that I could not see.

I somersaulted the living line
and found my New Arcadia in you,
and have allowed an ecumenicism of the ages,
in tribute to all those in history
who knew, believed what I now do,
who struggled, were persecuted, suffered
because they knew what I now know
and believed in what I believe,
in the ether of those ages,
in this place of peace, now mine.

355. In Faith

I am building my tower, Lord,
with 365 boards,
that lift it high,
so others can read it,
so, in faith, that I can complete it,
and that you could say, "This one began to build,
but *did* have resources to finish."

I am almost there
and when I finish there will be
a tower of words
that, in faith, will not diminish.
I lift the words up to you
as my frankincense and myrrh,
my mark for others to see.
    From Luke 14:30

356. Silent Night

Lord,
On this holy night we gather.
We can feel you here
and the world over, we enjoy,
we gather and sing
your praises and celebrate
the most important night of all,
the night in Bethlehem
when God became a boy.

We come and worship you,
Christ the Lord,
the children, parents and elders,
alive on this night so right, so near,
we hold hands and bring
gifts of love and adoration,
the lamplight of your love will unfurl
and when we leave we hear
the voices of the choir sing
"Joy to the World."

357. Should Not Be Forgotten

Lord Jesus,
Joseph could have said no
to Mary and not believe
she had been visited by your father.

He could have said no,
as could many today,
but what do they have
to offer as their "yes"?

He took a leap
in believing her story
of your birth to be begotten,
so now her story is your story and ours,
and what Joseph did
should not be forgotten.

358. Christmas

Lord, Emmanuel,
The cold night measures closer each hour
to the time when the world over
we think of birth, hope, possibility,
heavenly might
that we can now all live without uselessness
instead blank slates where holy codes are written,
and death is a closed door
but instead live with you, through you,
not alone
and your flesh-word with open doors
long ago promised in a starlit night.

359. O, Paul

O, Paul,
You brightest flame
of Christ's fire,
what would we
have done without you?
You sold the Word
like no other,
teaching all of us, then and now
so many lessons,
we should all be at want
without them because
of all the Apostles, you showed us how.

O, Paul,
Through the ages in our readings
we've heard your call,
begging us to follow the Lord,
to keep our faith
and that this is what matters most.
I pray that all will make attempts
to measure up to your holy pleadings.
Amen.

360. O, Peter

O, Peter,
Christ's lieutenant,
Apostle most like us,
fallible, afraid at times,
but more than any you had purpose,
to persuade thousands to follow our Lord,
and more than most you paid
your price when you were captured
and crucified upside down
in Nero's Circus,
because in much grand gesture
of your holy humility,
your representative humanity,
you did not in any way want
your ending to be compared
to the Holy One you sacrificed
yourself to promote.

361. At Least Mostly

She sits in the overflow area
in the parking lot for those waiting
in the terminal terminal
and, by your grace, Lord,
she is proportionally absent
of who, where and when she is,
accepting of it, at least mostly
and so has been relieved
of some of her virtues of earlier days
into a peaceful, at least mostly,
sanctum of the wreckage of age
yet lovely in her ways.

Lord,
protect the aged and the child,
whoever, however, whenever they may be,
they are more deserving,
at least mostly

of access to your eternity
and when the time does come,
let them cross the night river, safely,
into your arms,
O Lord.

362. Transformation 1: Grape to Wine

Lord,
You gave us grapes
with clusters like earrings on vines,
you gave us the understanding
of transforming the grapes to juice,
and then you placed your spark
into it and it ignited into wine,
transforming itself the way you did
when you defied death
and put the spark in us.

From eras ancient or nigh,
in Egypt with Moses,
in Greece with Pericles,
in Rome with Caesar,
whose legions carried
the seeds with them
wherever they went.
This liquid art you even
shared in your Last Supper,
and some of us know why.

363. Transformation 2: Flour, Water to Bread

Lord,
Flower and water
are just that, flour and water,
unleavened, without their soul.
We add yeast and then
they rise from the dead,
just as you did, Lord,
and with heat transform into bread,

the way you rose when hundreds saw you
and raced to tell hundreds more,
then thousands more yet,
so that the rising of your word,
what you did and said
for all the people, your giving,
traveled like pollen across the earth,
just as did the risen bread,
become the colossal staple of the living.

364. Transformation 3: Clay/Heat to Pottery

Lord, How so long ago it was,
when your people put clay into a fire
and were endowed with its transformation
from one material into another,
like you did in your resurrection,
and you are the heat that bonds,
that allows us to make better endurance
of the struggles of the breathing,
and to make implements for eating, lighting,
as the clay lamps did in your home,
Lord, when you were a boy.

365. The Last Prayer

I'm at the line's end, Lord,
after a succession of days,
some which passed like quicksilver rhythms,
some which crawled with inch worm speed traveling a leaf.
Days in prayer, recognition
of your peace when knowing, Lord,
that you are our invisible jolt,
a corpuscle catapult that you ignite,
your trust thrusts,
even to those unknowingly participating
in your wattage in house, room, cottage,
you are, as usual, there,
out of sight but not body.

www.ingramcontent.com/pod-product-compliance
Lightning Source LLC
Chambersburg PA
CBHW060604230426
43670CB00011B/1960